Felipe Solís

NATIONAL MUSEUM
OF ANTHROPOLOGY

238 color photos

MONCLEM
EDICIONES

BONECHI

CONTENTS

INTRODUCTION

An extraordinary nucleus of high civilization arose in the second millennium B.C. in a wide area of Mexico and Central America that was baptized Mesoamerica around the middle of this century. By tradition, the region has kept this name until today although the concept of this large cultural area, whose boundaries constantly changed in the course of the pre-Hispanic and Colonial periods, has varied. The cultural development of Mesoamerica ended with the Spanish Conquest of the entire area which began in 1521 when Tenochtitlán, the Aztec capital was taken and ended in 1697 with the fall of Ta Itzá in the heart of the Maya rain forest.

More than a geographical area, Mesoamerica is a cultural concept, since different ethnic groups speaking numerous languages developed in it who created different cultures but were all united by a similar concept of the world and of life. This led them to identify with one another in many aspects, both economically, politically and socially, as well as in various cultural creations. The main groups were the Olmecs, a people of unknown identity, whose principal territory was southern Veracruz and northern Tabasco, but who spread all over Mesoamerica long before the Christian era. This is demonstrated by the existence of great cities in other regions such as Teopantecuanitlán in Guerrero and Chalcatzingo in Morelos. The Mayas, made up of some 28 ethnic groups, each speaking a different language, who lived in southeast Mexico and various Central American countries (Guatemala, Belize and parts of Honduras and El Salvador), the masters of advanced scientific knowledge and creators of magnificent plastic art with a remarkable humanistic sense. The inhabitants of Teotihuacán (whose language and name are still unknown), builders of the first great city on the Central Plateau of Mexico and also creators of important cultural traditions. The Nahuas, who received the heritage of Teotihuacán, particularly the Aztecs who established a great empire that began with the foundation of Tenochtitlán (1325 A.D.) in the lake of Texcoco. The Zapotecs and Mixtecs, living in the regions that now make up the state of Oaxaca; the Totonacs of central Veracruz, the Tarascans of the present-day state of Michoacán, and many others.

After the beginning of agriculture, with corn as the main product, numerous population centers grew up all over Mesoamerica, many of which achieved such a degree of development that they can be considered real urban nuclei. Mesoamerican cities possess one or more centers where their main buildings stood. These include pyramidal bases to support temples and house burials, courts for the ballgame, which was one of the major rites, and dwelling complexes for the ruling classes. These centers were conceived as microcosms which reproduced the great levels of the universe and functioned as axis mundi from where communication was made with the sacred energies, manifested in beings and forces of nature, led by the sun, which governed the lives of these peoples. But in large cities there were also hundreds of civil buildings: dwelling complexes, markets and others that tell us about social hierarchies and the ways of community life.

One of the most notable features of Mesoamerican cultures is their consciousness of history, which is shown in their eagerness to preserve the memory of the past in codices painted on bark paper or deerskin, and inscriptions carved in stone or stucco. For this they invented several writing systems, of which the most important is the Maya one because it is the most evolved, which is why it has not been possible to decipher it fully. Writing was also used to describe the myths and rites of their complex religion and record scientific knowledge such as mathematics, astronomy and chronology. These systems, whose first indications are found in a wide region lying between the Olmec area on the Gulf Coast of Mexico and El Salvador developed remarkably in the Maya area, where a complex calendar system was created to record dates with extreme accuracy, thanks to the concept of zero and the positional value of numerical signs, invented in the 5th century B.C. A great cultural legacy of Mesoamerican peoples has been recovered: cities, innumerable objects — some of which are extraordinary works of art — and a few codices. A fundamental part of this heritage is preserved in the National Museum of Anthropology in Mexico City, giving the present-day world and that of the future a picture of ancient Mexican Indian cultures as well as of their descendents who in some way or other have kept alive the old concept of the world and life.

Mercedes de la Garza
Director of the National Museum
of Anthropology

Esplanade leading to the entrance of the National Museum of Anthropology. On the marble facade there is the National Coat of Arms: an eagle perched on a cactus, devouring a serpent, an emblem of pre-Hispanic origin.

Right. Overall view of the monumental patio inside the Museum with its enormous umbrella roof and pool with lotuses and papyrus where there is also the metal shell with a clock inside that signals the passing of the hours with the sound of conch trumpets.

In the outside fountain of the Museum is the monumental statue of a Rain god in volcanic stone, generally known as Tláloc. From Coatlinchán, State of Mexico.

THE NATIONAL MUSEUM OF ANTHROPOLOGY

The modern building of the National Museum of Anthropology was opened in Chapultepec Park on September 17, 1964. With all the technical and museological advances of its time, it was designed to show the origin, evolution and contributions of pre-Hispanic civilizations and also the typical way of life and culture of Mexico's ethnic groups.

After long years of research and preparation for the project, the architect Pedro Ramírez Vázquez together with a team of architects, museographers and investigators, plus several hundred manual workers and builders, in 18 months of hard work were able to raise this magnificent building which covers 45,000 square meters and is still one of the most outstanding museum facilities in the world. The exhibition halls surround a spacious patio where visitors can appreciate a large pool and the impressive umbrella roof.

With the discovery of the monolithic statue of the goddess Coatlicue on August 13, 1790, when Mexico was still part of the Spanish Empire, and the wise decision of the viceroy, the Count of Revillagigedo, to send this important find for safekeeping in the courtyard of the old university located on premises south of the Viceregal Palace, Mexico's custom of protecting its cultural heritage was born. In this way, the University Museum was created, the first such institution in the country. In December 1790 the Sun Stone was discovered, whose fate was different, since it was placed on public view at the base of the southwest tower of Mexico City cathedral.

In the course of time, the archaeological finds, consisting of sculptures, pottery, figurines, etc. constantly being made in the valley and Mexico City accumulated

in this first Museum. However, in 1825, the first president of Mexico, Guadalupe Victoria, issued a decree creating the National Museum which, like many museums of the time around the world, housed carriages, pictures, documents, flags, etc. that illustrated Mexico's recent past. The budding institution, in addition to the archaeological pieces discovered, also contained examples of the country's natural history.

In 1865, during his short-lived empire, Maximilian of Hapsburg ordered the location of the Museum to be changed because of the need for more space. He granted the old Mint for the purpose, where precious metals were smelted and coins struck in the Colonial era. It was a beautiful palace dating from the time of Philip V, located in the large block of buildings attached to the National Palace in the Historical Center of Mexico City. The great monoliths were taken there and placed in the courtyard; in the rooms the archaeology, geology, zoology, and other collections, as well as furniture and documents from the Colonial period and the time of the War of Independence were arranged in chronological sequence.

That old Museum was a fruitful place for the growth of knowledge about ancient pre-Hispanic Mexican cultures and the study of the country's history. It was here that some of the foremost researchers of their time were trained, since in this atmosphere conducive to the appreciation of the ancient indigenous world the most important museum related event of the 19th century took place: the inauguration of the "Monolith Hall" by President Porfirio Díaz in 1887. The monumental sculptures, silent witnesses of the country's different native cultures, were placed haphazardly without any chronological sequence In the largest room of the building, where gold and silver used to be smelted at one time. In the center of the Hall stood the imposing Sun Stone which from then on became the symbol of pre-Hispanic Indian Mexico.

In the early decades of the 20th century, with the scientific advances made in anthropology and archaeology, chronologies were refined, which made it possible to situate the different ethnic cultures in time and space. In addition, academic criteria were defined for displaying the finest cultural and artistic testimonials of pre-Hispanic peoples in the most appropriate manner. As a result, by the middle of this century, the Na-

On one side of the Museum's entrance hall is the mural by Rufino Tamayo showing the struggle between the forces of night and day, symbolized by the gods Quetzalcóatl and Tezcatlipoca.

Decoration on the outside of the Ethnography Rooms on the upper floor of the Museum. This aluminum grille by Manuel Felguérez evokes undulating serpents similar to Maya decoration on Puuc style buildings.

tional Museum of Anthropology, from which the objects related to natural history and national history had been removed previously, proudly exhibited its archaeological and ethnological collections.

With its move to Chapultepec Park in 1964, studies and museography for the new Museum determined that the pre-Hispanic cultures would occupy the lower floor in twelve Rooms beginning with two orientation spaces: Introduction to Anthropology and Mesoamerica. The Origins Room was located next, devoted to Mexican Prehistory. These are followed in evolutionary and chronological order by the Pre-Classic, Teotihuacán and Toltec Rooms, which show the different developmental stages of the peoples who lived on the Central Plateau. After these come another five Rooms where visitors can see the artistic and cultural testimonials of the inhabitants of other regions of Mesoamerica: the Oaxaca, Gulf Coast, Maya, North and West Mexico Rooms.

The ten Rooms on the upper floor were dedicated to illustrating the culture of the largest contemporary indigenous groups in the country: the Introduction to Ethnology; Coras and Huichols; Purépechas (Tarascans); Otomis; Northern Sierra de Puebla; Oaxaca; Huastecs and Totonacs; Highland and Lowland Mayas, and groups of the Northwest.

This mural by Jorge González Camarena illustrates the anthropological concept of the unity and variety of humankind. Numerous female figures show that human beings, no matter the color of their skin, stature or physical appearance, belong to one great family.

INTRODUCTION TO ANTHROPOLOGY

The first Room in the Museum, which is on the right-hand side of the patio where the giant umbrella roof stands, shows us the content and characteristics of anthropology, a social science which seeks the comprehensive knowledge of man, and whose objective is to provide elements for understanding humankind with its individual and collective characteristics.

Visitors are welcomed by the mural by Jorge González Camarena, in which both the unity and variety of the human race are illustrated with great luminosity and harmonious composition. The message of this work is deep, demonstrating that all men, regardless of race or color, have the same right to exist, and that their cultural tokens are the best proof of this statement. In this Room, we can appreciate the kinship between the peoples of pre-Hispanic Mexico and its present-day ethnic groups and all the world.

Anthropology is made up of several sciences, and the Room illustrates four of the most important: physical anthropology, archaeology, linguistics and ethnography. Thanks to the varied elements of the exhibition, visitors can become familiar with the contents and purposes of these disciplines.

The first part shows the major issues of the evolution of life on earth. Using original fossils and reproductions, bone remains and other objects, the presence of the first living creatures which arose millions of years ago is explained, with special emphasis on mammals, the last to appear. The evolutionary process of man is also shown in detail, with displays of the most famous finds of prehominid, hominid and prehistoric

View of the central section of the Mesoamerica Room, where the large mural by José Chávez Morado describes the process followed by the peoples of ancient Mexico in the growth of Mesoamerican civilization, from hunting and gathering to the emergence of the great cultures.

human remains, the most important of these being Neanderthal and Cro-Magnon man. The public is introduced to physical anthropology by means of an ample description. Osteology enables us to distinguish differences in the skeletal structure of men and women, and by studying these we can determine ages and anomalous features. Specialists in human remains have been able to identify the beauty practices of times gone by: cranial deformation and dental mutilation are those most easily recognized. To understand the unity and variety of the human race, this science shows us the characteristic features of each one of the groups scattered over the world: the great height of African Zulus and the steatopygia of the women of this continent; the almond-shaped eyes of the inhabitants of China, Japan and Manchuria and the Mongolian spot typical of these peoples, which also appears among the indigenous groups of America, due to the fact that the settlers of this region come mainly from northern Asia.

Archaeology is the scientific study of human societies in the past through the analysis of their material remains. In the corresponding section of this Room, the excavation techniques used by archaeologists are explained, and the careful extraction of their finds makes it possible to determine the succession of cultures by means of stratigraphy. A comparative table of the main ancient cultures of the world places the inhabitants of pre-Hispanic Mexico alongside the Egyptians, Mesopotamians and the peoples of India.

The different interesting archaeological objects, especially silex axes, funerary masks, oil vessels, sarcophagi, ancient inscriptions, etc. show the evolution of man's material culture since prehistory to the flowering of the first civilizations.

The exhibition showing the elements that linguistics

works with occupies the center of the Room. This explains how human communication works in its different forms: written and spoken language, with all their variables, to which music can also be added, accounting for the presence of curious instruments to produce musical sounds.

The section devoted to ethnography rounds off the visit. This displays many objects made by various peoples in different parts of the world. These show how man finds similar or different solutions to the problems of adapting to life in diverse environments. Thus, human culture is a constant process of invention and creation making use of the resources at hand.

MESOAMERICA

In 1964, when the Museum was inaugurated, the term Mesoamerica — which describes the cultural macroarea where remarkable civilizations developed, covering most of Mexico and extending into neighboring Central American countries — was widely accepted among anthropologists. It was Paul Kirchhoff,

a renowned German anthropologist resident in Mexico who after many years of patient investigation proposed this identification, based on the study of different culture traits.

Kirchhoff suggests that by the 16th century, according to information provided in the many chronicles and histories written after the Spanish Conquest, northern Mexico differed considerably from the center and south. This was because the peoples living in the latter areas had attained a high level of technical and artistic knowledge. The area extended beyond the frontiers of Mexico, covering also Guatemala, Belize, El Salvador and part of Honduras and Costa Rica. This is why it is called Mesoamerica.

This second introductory Room of the Museum is devoted to showing the culture traits that define Mesoamerica, interpreted by the painter Luis Covarrubias in a multicolored map where visitors can see the limits of this macroarea. Thanks to the definition of topographical relief and the main geographical features, the environmental variants can be understood better. In his work, Covarrubias used the finest archaeological pieces from the different pre-Hispanic cultures exhibited in the Museum to situate them in

Iker Larrauri pictured the moment when man crossed over from Asia to America with his few belongings. According to archaeologists, this can be dated to around 80,000 years ago.

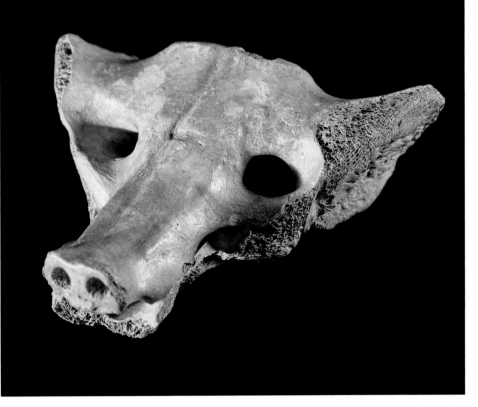

The most remarkable prehistoric work of art is the Tequixquiac Sacrum, a mask of a coyote made from the bone of a llama, a now extinct animal that once existed in Mexico.

such a complex geographical environment. There are Mayas, Olmecs, Mixtecs and Zapotecs; Totonacs and Huastecs; Mexicas, Teotihuacans, Toltecs, and finally Purépechas, each group in its region.

A visit to this Room reveals how all Mesoamerican peoples engaged in intensive agriculture, growing the plants that enabled them to advance their civilizations, especially corn. For this, they developed a complex system that included irrigation channels, terraces and *chinampas* ("floating gardens"). For planting, they had digging sticks known as coas and in later times copper and bronze hoes.

Since they had no large animals they could raise, they were only able to domesticate turkeys and dogs and so had to supplement their economy by hunting, fishing and collecting. They used all kinds of weapons and tools for this, particularly the atlatl or spear-thrower that enabled them to shoot further and more accurately.

Although all pre-Hispanic peoples in general came mainly from northern Asia they tried to set themselves apart physically with their own beautifying practices, in particular cranial deformation of various types, tooth filing, scarification, etc. The sculptures, reliefs and figurines of this Room demonstrate the identity that each culture sought for itself by way of special clothing, elegant body ornaments, hairstyles and the deformations mentioned above.

A mural by José Chávez Moreno in the upper part of the Room illustrates the evolution of Mesoamerican peoples and cultures. This is supplemented by many archaeological objects under glass domes on pedestals or in showcases: pottery in the styles of each region, together with ornaments of shell, jade, turquoise, obsidian and the precious metals they favored.

In the final section of the Room, cultural strides forward are represented by pictographic writing; the solar calendar of 365 days and the ritual one of 260 days. The tradition of producing picture books, codices, on bark paper or strips of deerskin; the refined tech-

Remains of a mammoth discovered in Santa Isabel Ixtapan near Texcoco. These prove that the animal was brought down by a group of hunters who left behind points of the weapons used to attack it.

niques of lapidaries, metal workers and other specialist craftsmen who contributed their work to the magnificence of capital cities adorned with stone carvings, reliefs and brightly colored murals all together illustrate the cultural unity of Mesoamerica.

Monumental architecture is the most attractive feature of Mexico, and the Room contains scale models of some pyramids, including the Pyramid of the Sun in Teotihuacán, the circular base of Cuicuilco, the Aztec Great Temple, etc. Visitors can compare their volume and dimensions, and at the same time these models are an invitation to visit the original constructions located on different archaeological sites in Mesoamerica.

ORIGINS

The prehistoric era of the American continent, in particular Mexico, is relatively recent in comparison with that of the Old World. It covers a period of no more than 80,000 years, and to this we must add the fact that man did not originate in America. This stage is the object of painstaking research by specialists in human and animal remains, and although there are not the sensational finds so often made in Africa and Asia dating back to our remotest ancestors millions of years ago, it is considered to belong to the origins of man.

At the entrance to this room is a mural by Iker Larrauri showing a panoramic scene of hunters coming from Asia to follow the migrations and movement of large mammals over the Bering Straits. In the distance, the tip of Alaska covered with glaciers is both a challenge and an invitation to discover new lands.

Numerous drawings and maps explain when the glaciers grew that covered the north of the Earth with ice and created a bridge between Asia and America which has been named Beringia. This was temporarily the way for human migrations which must have taken place more than 80,000 years ago. This popula-

Six thousand years before our era the lake basin of the Valley of Mexico met the environmental conditions for Pleistocene animals, especially mammoths. The hunters of the time attacked these huge beasts as they floundered in the mud.

tion movement was in waves, and this is why the different groups, over the course of thousands of years, finally reached the extreme south of the American continent. The Eskimos were the last group to enter the northern area, where they continue to live until today.

The first part of the Room shows the oldest stage of hunter-gatherers in Mexico. The diorama shows the difficult living conditions on rock ledges or in caves where they sheltered from the weather. Their basic knowledge was confined to making fire and chipping rough tools out of stone to serve as axes, hammers, rasps and scrapers.

In a well at the center of the room are the original bones of the mammoth discovered at Santa Isabel Ixtapan in 1954. A showcase at one side holds stone tools which are evidence that no more than 10,000 years ago in the Valley of Mexico, man was killing these enormous animals when he found them trapped in the mud of lake sides. Another diorama shows a hunting scene in Tepexpan, where the remains of a mammoth were discovered in 1947, with a group of hunters engaged in their difficult task.

A large mural in this same section of the Room illustrates what is known as Pleistocene fauna, consisting of many animals that have become extinct but were hunted for food by the settlers of the New World. The bones exhibited here include the "Sacro de Tequix-

quiac" (Tequixquiac Sacrum) from a fossilized llama made into a mask by prehistoric man which is Mexico's most ancient work of art.

Thanks to the skeletal remains of ancient man that have been recovered we can reconstruct his physical appearance, know how tall he grew, the ailments he suffered from, and so on. This Room also displays some of the best preserved skulls of the ancient settlers of the Central Plateau of Mexico, whose approximate age can be ascertained by applying the carbon 14 technique. The most important items on display are the skull of Peñón man and the one from Santa María Astahuacán, both discovered in the Valley of Mexico and both 8,000 years old, while from the state of Puebla are the Coxcatlán skull between 6,800 and 5,000 years old and the one from El Texcal, 5,000 years old.

The last section illustrates the process of domesticating food plants, especially corn, which gave birth to the first developmental stage of Mesoamerica: agricultural societies. The diorama at the end of the Room recreates a settlement in the Valley of Tehuacán between 3400 and 2300 B.C. showing sedentarization, with corn crops and underground dwellings. People of this time already used irrigation to obtain better harvests. The most commonly used utensils were grindstones and mortars, in Mexico known as metates and molcajetes.

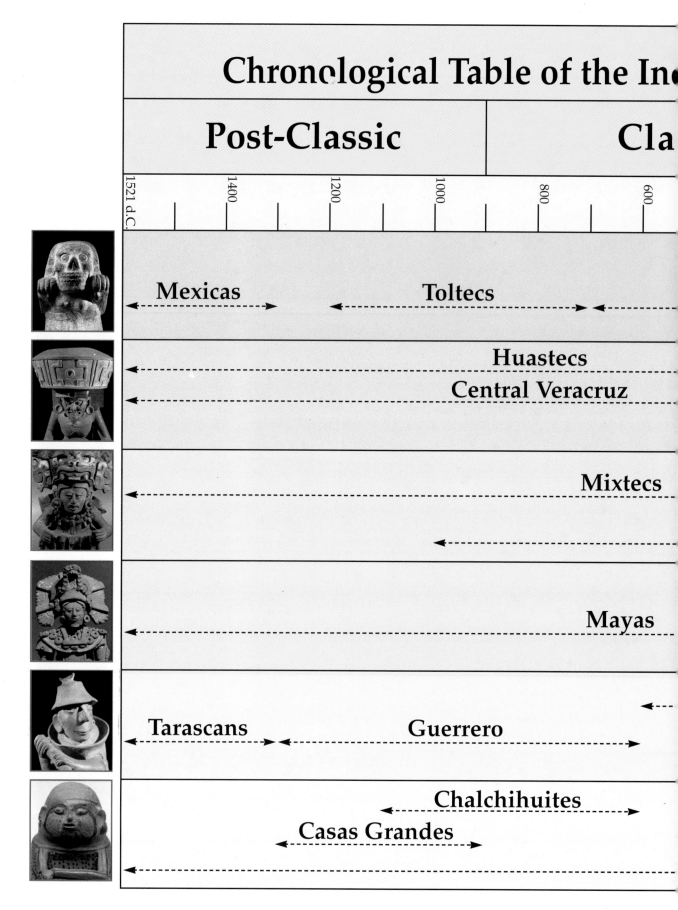

Chronological Table of the In⟨

Post-Classic		Cla

1521 d.C.　1400　1200　1000　800　600

Mexicas ←----→　←---------- Toltecs ---------→　←----

Huastecs ←----------------
Central Veracruz ←----------------

Mixtecs ←----------------

←----------------

Mayas ←----------------

←---

Tarascans ←----→　←---------- Guerrero ----------→

Chalchihuites ←----------→
Casas Grandes ←----------→

←----------------

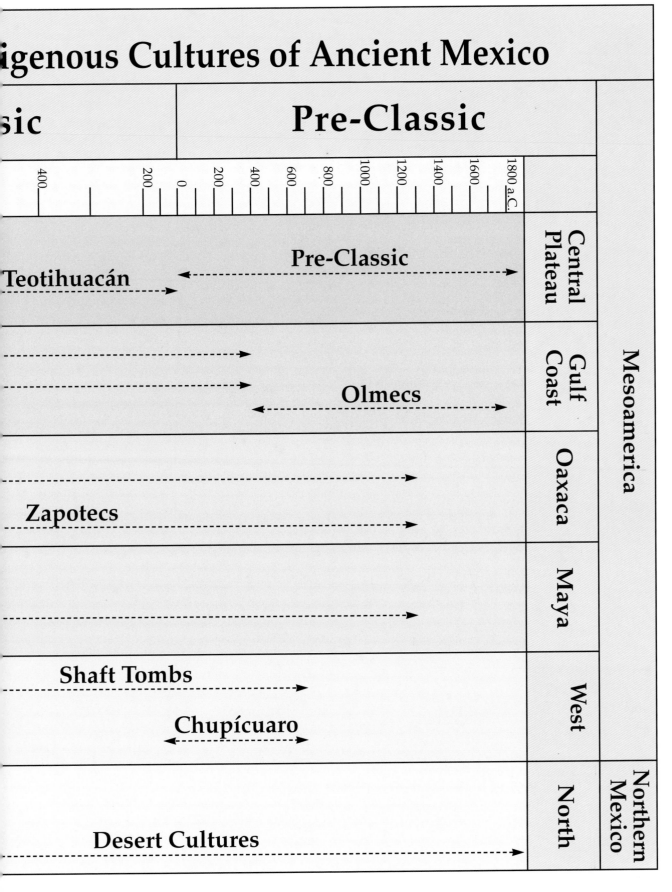

igenous Cultures of Ancient Mexico

sic	Pre-Classic

400 | 200 | 0 | 200 | 400 | 600 | 800 | 1000 | 1200 | 1400 | 1600 | 1800 a.C.

Pre-Classic

Teotihuacán

Olmecs

Zapotecs

Shaft Tombs

Chupícuaro

Desert Cultures

Central Plateau

Gulf Coast

Oaxaca

Maya

West

North

Mesoamerica

Northern Mexico

PRE-CLASSIC

The Central Plateau of Mexico is the area of Meso-america to which four consecutive Rooms are dedicated, to illustrate the evolutionary process of the peoples and cultures that developed in the region. The Pre-Classic Room shows the first agricultural societies on the Central Plateau, dating from 2500 to 100 B.C. Today, thanks to archaeological studies, we know that this long period was divided into two major stages: the emergence of the first settlements, some of which eventually became great ceremonial centers as a result of their economic and social success. With the appearance of these, the second stage began.

The Central Plateau of Mexico is characterized by large valleys surrounded by high mountains rising to a maximum of 1,000 meters above sea level, by numerous rivers and streams, by extensive lakes that had existed since prehistoric times where there was abundant animal life. This, in addition to a wealth of trees and plants, made the region very attractive as a place to live.

The economy of these early societies was mixed. It was based mainly on the intensive cultivation of different food plants, especially corn, beans, squash and chillies, supplemented by abundant products from hunting and fishing which supplied animal protein, and by the collecting of all types of wild plants and seeds. Even today, as an inheritance of this adaptation to the environment, Mexicans are fond of including both animals and plants in their popular dishes that are completely unknown in other countries.

The major human settlements were located on the flanks of mountains, around lake basins and on riverbanks. The most notable of these are the ones that have been studied by archaeologists in the enormous area now covered by Mexico City. These are Ticomán,

El Arbolillo and Zacatenco in the northern area, Tlatilco in the west of the valley, Cuicuilco in the south, and Tlapacoya in the east.

On these sites, it has been discovered that the ancient pre-Classic inhabitants used to build their houses of mud, wood and dry grass next to their fields. As each settlement grew in power and wealth, the custom arose of erecting ceremonial buildings in the form of pyramidal bases topped by temples. Architects, basing themselves on precise astronomical observations, planned population centers with a particular urban concept: squares surrounded by these ritual buildings with residential complexes on the outskirts. From the very beginning, the custom existed of burying the dead underneath the floor of their homes.

Nowadays, these burials are our main cultural evidence from those times. The great attraction of this Room is the exhibition of one of these burial complexes from the excavations at Tlatilco. It illustrates the custom of accompanying the dead with rich offerings of pottery vessels and figurines showing the shapes and decorative elements that were the dominant style of the time. The elegant water pourers and vessels in the shape of animals and plants are particularly remarkable.

The lovely figures and figurines, especially the human ones, illustrate the beauty standards of the past: women associated with the cult of the mother goddess, obese individuals that show influence from the Gulf Coast Olmecs, strange figures with two heads or faces that point to the duality of the universe.

With the emergence of the first ceremonial centers came the worship of the first gods: Huehuetéotl, the Old God of Fire, represented as an old man in a seated position with a brazier on his back and associated with the fire from the volcanoes. Tláloc, god of Rain whose primitive image — a head with long hair, bulging eyes and enormous canine teeth — appeared on certain sacred vessels.

MEXICO

GULF OF MEXICO

PACIFIC OCEAN

CENTRAL PLATEAU

PRE-CLASSIC

Right. Hollow figurine from Atlihuayán, Morelos, of a fat-cheeked person wearing a cape evoking a fantastic animal with jaguar and lizard characteristics. It is considered one of the best examples of Olmec influence on the Central High Plateau of Mexico.

Elegant vessel from Tlatilco in the shape of a fish. An example of how the pre-Classic inhabitants reproduced elements of their environment.

Right. Above left. The concept of duality grew up in the Middle pre-Classic (1500-600 B.C.) which would govern the religious ideology of the pre-Hispanic world. The female figurines with two heads are particularly significant.

Right. Above right. Some curious figurines show another interpretation of duality: a single head with two faces and three eyes like this one also from Tlatilco.

Right. Below left. Potter-artists of the pre-Classic era demonstrated great creativity in crafting female figurines like this dancer wearing a distinctive short skirt. Tlatilco.

Right. Below right. The clay female figurines are thought to be collective images of the cult to Mother Nature, combining the fertility of the earth with that of women. Therefore, many of them are shown carrying a child.

Zoomorphic bottle representing an armadillo discovered in the excavations of Tlatilco, State of Mexico. Additional decoration to the graceful molding is the incised design of curves on the animal's shell.

Archaeological material from some pre-Classic villages such as Gualupita in the State of Morelos includes hollow clay figurines of stylized fat-cheeked individuals resembling the "baby-face" pieces of the Olmecs.

Above left. The figurines of women kissing or nursing dogs are striking. These were probably the hairless breed called xoloitzcuintli which reminded them of small children.

In Cuicuilco, in the south of the Valley of Mexico there arose the worship of Huehuetéotl, the god of Fire, represented by an old man carrying a receptacle or brazier on his back which symbolizes volcano cones and fire from the earth.

Strong influence from the Olmec world of the Gulf coast can be
seen at the archaeological site of Gualupita. The finest
example of artistic production is this fragment of a "baby-face"
figurine with an enigmatic expression which still has white
kaolin on its face contrasting with the red that symbolizes hair.

One of the burials discovered during excavations at Tlatilco contained the offering of this striking vessel in the shape of a contortionist. This gives researchers the idea that the buried person may have been a shaman.

Right. The concept of duality in the pre-Classic era is also expressed by this small clay mask from Tlatilco. Half of the face is lively, with the tongue out, while the other half is a fleshless skull.

TEOTIHUACAN

This Room shows all the splendor of the first city to arise in Mesoamerica: Teotihuacán, whose name means "the place where gods are born." This city grew over the period from 100 B.C. to 650-750 A.D. which researchers define as the Classic era. Its origins date back to the terrible destruction in the south of the valley caused by the volcanic eruption that destroyed Cuicuilco and led to a great migration into the northeast of the valley where the displaced population united with several villages and finally gave rise to this magnificent city.

A scale model shows the characteristics of this native capital, with its main thoroughfare, the Avenue of the Dead running north to south. Because of ritual requirements for celebrating the equinoxes this was given a deviation of 17° west. At its height — around the 6th century — the city covered more than 50 square kilometers. It was basically divided into quadrants or large sectors containing both ceremonial complexes and so-called palaces which are actually living quarters. Today, only the core of the city stands, with the Pyramid of the Sun, the Pyramid of the Moon, the Ciudadela (Citadel) and some palaces with their patios and rooms.

Archaeologists have identified four stages in the city's evolution. These we know especially from the different types of pottery, by the technology and the iconography of figurines which together with the various buildings uncovered since the beginning of this century, allows us to date them.

The showcases in the first two sections of the Room illustrate the changes that occurred both in the shapes of vessels and the way they were decorated in the course of 7 or 8 centuries. The most outstanding feature is what is known as "fine orange ware" that was a basic element in Teotihuacán's trade. At the same time, it can be seen that the tripod vessels with vertical sides were an identifying mark of the capital and its inhabitants, who occasionally decorated their pottery using the fresco technique similar to the one they employed in their mural paintings.

Another crucial item in their world of trade was obsidian, whose mining and distribution was almost exclusively theirs. This allowed them to obtain valuable raw materials from other regions of Mesoamerica which led them to dominate many different peoples. The many facets of technology are shown in the Room, explaining how they constructed buildings, made pottery, produced ornaments and instruments of shell and bone, sculpted remarkable monoliths out of volcanic stone or carved the famous funerary masks in diorite, alabaster and other veined stones that are considered to be their most exquisite artistic expressions.

In the central part of the Room a large mural by Nicolás Moreno places us in the Valley of Teotihuacán. Its perspective leads visitors into the distant Valley of Mexico wrapped in a summer storm. And it is here that the grandiose architecture of the city is brought out with a reproduction of the facade of the Pyramid of the Plumed Serpents framed by carefully selected samples of sculpture and mural paintings — an invitation to complement a visit to the museum with a trip to the archaeological site a short distance away from Mexico City.

The Room closes with an imposing group of three ritual funerary sculptures that were part of the Late pre-Classic decoration of the Pyramid of the Sun: a stone disk with a human skull in relief in the center, accompanied by two carvings in high relief also of human skulls, images which signify the death of the sun in the west of the universe and in the Room symbolize the end of Teotihuacán civilization, which happened around the 7th century A.D.

Right. A notable find from the state of Guerrero illustrating Teotihuacán's influence in the region is this mask carved in volcanic stone covered with bluish-green turquoise mosaic. The stylized eyebrows, the flower in the center of the forehead and the nose ornament in the shape of a stepped fret are of red shell.

The monumental sculpture in volcanic stone of a goddess identified as Chalchiuhtlicue, the patroness of Water, is the main feature in the central section of the Teotihuacán Room.

The inhabitants of Teotihuacán produced clay masks cast in molds which had the main place on scenic braziers. This example, one of the finest in existence, has color on the face representing makeup and in addition sports an elegant curved feather.

One of the most important structures in
Teotihuacán is the Pyramid of Quetzalcóatl. A
full-sized glass fiber replica of one corner with
all its original color stands in this room. An
imposing series of undulating serpents that
emerge from a wall like a feather flower and
have a mask on their backs.

The inhabitants of Teotihuacán created an
unmistakable style in their funerary masks, repeating
the pattern of an idealized youthful human face. This
example has three bands over the mouth, nose and
eyes in turquoise and shell mosaic.

31

Of all the pottery produced in Teotihuacán the straight sided tripod bowls were the most original. Some of them were decorated with fresco painting like that of murals. This one shows an elaborately dressed warrior holding an obsidian knife with a heart on it.

Clay mask made with different molds showing the ornaments worn by the elegant men of Teotihuacán: large round ear spools and stylized butterfly nose plugs.

The lapidaries of the Classic world looked for green or gray veined stone to produce idealized images of human beings, which were given life by embedding a bead inside as a heart.

This large terra-cotta figure was discovered at Xolalpan, near Teotihuacán. It represents a warrior or priest of the cult to Xipe-Totec and so is wearing the skin of a sacrificially flayed victim over the face and part of the body. He is holding a shield and a vessel shaped like a jaguar claw.

Left. Above left. Teotihuacán tripod vessels show different decorative techniques. On this piece there is a combination of small molded applications for the lower band in contrast to the cut-out panels with designs of interlaced volutes on the sides. The lid is topped by the figure of a bird.

Left. Above right. Nanchititla is the small locality in the State of Mexico where this vase carved of green stone was found. It represents a water god which may be a version of Tláloc or Cocijo, the Zapotec god of Rain.

Although no ballcourts have been discovered at Teotihuacán, targets used in this ritual sport do exist. This example from La Ventilla is made up of four separately carved stone sections decorated with curved braids. The disk symbolizes movement.

Left. Below left. Some of the clay figurines from Teotihuacán combine modeling and molding. This highly original one has another small image inside, which has been interpreted as a metaphor for motherhood or the alter ego.

Left. Below right. The people of Teotihuacán were very fond of making molded clay figurines with articulated limbs, leading some researchers to believe they are puppets.

The Pyramid of the Sun at Teotihuacán once had a facade decorated with symbols of death. This is the origin of this fragment of a disk with a human skull in the center showing its tongue. Its nimbus seems to be a large bow of pleated paper.

Left. The typical ritual vessels of Teotihuacán were clay braziers requiring the production of many different parts in molds. These were later applied to the whole vessel to form a scene. This piece pays homage to quetzals and butterflies.

Clay bowl in the shape of a reclining ballgame player wearing a kind of protective skirt with a curved protuberance on the front and a disk at the hip.

A unique ceramic piece of an imaginary bird decorated with necklaces of cut shells and conches, jade eyes and a crest of red shells. Popularly known as "The Crazy Hen."

TOLTEC

There was a deep change in all the cultural fields of central Mesoamerica after Teotihuacán was abandoned, and the Toltec Room reflects them in the cities that flourished from 700 to 1300 A.D. This comprises two periods that archaeologists have named Epiclassic and Early post-Classic. The first of these is exemplified by the archaeological sites of Cacaxtla, Xochitécatl and Xochicalco. At the beginning of the Room there is a copy of the war murals in Cacaxtla, state of Tlaxcala, famous for its pictorial art. Xochitécatl is site that has come under archaeological study only recently where the curious figurines discovered are evidence of age-old female worship in Mesoamerica.

Xochicalco is given most weight in this part of the Room due to the fact that it was the most important capital of its time since it dominated the valleys of the state of Morelos. It was built on the top of three hills in a military style, where there were important cults to the feathered serpent and the principal stars. We can appreciate its wealth and power from the quality of its sculptures, the finest example of which is the head of a macaw, and in the contents of some offerings, which included objects from many different regions of Mesoamerica made of such attractive materials as alabaster, jade and shell.

The middle section of the Room contains objects from the Early post-Classic (900-1300 A.D.) when Tula, a city founded by Quetzalcóatl, dominated the Central Plateau of Mexico. Impressive because of its enormous dimensions is the column in the shape of a warrior, popularly known as an atlante from the Pyramid of Tlahuizcalpantecuhtli (Lord of the Morning Star) in the Toltec capital.

A tour begins with the mythological account of the struggle between Quetzalcóatl and Tezcatlipoca, gods who symbolize the confrontation of civilization and war. Following this is a picture by Luis Covarrubias of the central plaza in Tula at the time of its greatest splendor which illustrates the function and original position of the sculptures and reliefs exhibited at the sides. Other paintings by Alfredo Zalce show Quetzalcóatl as a man-god and the process of carving and erection Toltec artists had to undertake in producing the telamons (atlantes).

The ballgame, the main gods worshiped by the Toltecs and typical pottery vessels are displayed in the showcases that close this section. Here we can see that the shiny metallic plumbate pottery was the most in demand at the time because of its cost and beauty. The greatest treasure of this room is the head of a coyote made of plumbate ware and covered with mother-of-pearl mosaic.

The final section holds objects dating from the Mexica (Aztec) period discovered at Tula, especially clay bowls, incense burners and figurines that prove the presence of this people in the abandoned city of Quetzalcóatl. Visitors can also see the Toltec style warrior columns found in Mexico City, which underline the relationship between the two ancient capitals.

There is also the section devoted to the archaeological city of Teotenango, State of Mexico, with its vessels from the Matlatzinca culture, and the section on what is known as the "Culture of the Volcanoes." This consists of offerings made in honor of the god Tláloc that were discovered in shrines in the main heights of the eastern part of the Valley of Mexico.

The Toltec Room ends with archaeological pieces from Tenayuca, a site founded by Xólotl, chief of the Chichimecs, who brought new customs and culture traits to the Central Plateau, since this is the first double pyramid built, surrounded by a series of serpents.

Right. The inhabitants of Xochicalco in the state of Morelos worshiped the macaw, a form of the sun. This distinctive stone carving illustrates the quality of design achieved by Indian sculptors.

At Tula, temple roofs were supported by stone columns in the shape of warriors with their typical weapons and dress generally known as *atlantes*. One of these dominates the central part of the Toltec Room.

The plumbate ware typical of the Toltec era was a very important trade item, obtained from centers of production in Chiapas and Guatemala. This piece is a coyote with a lined face.

This painting by Alfredo Zalce in the Toltec Room shows the carving techniques used for the warrior columns and also the difficulties the builders had in taking the segments to the top of the pyramid where they stand.

Tláloc acquired great importance among the Toltecs as the god of Rain. This multicolored clay figurine shows the god's characteristic mask with eye rings and nose plug, and his elegant feather cape.

The inhabitants of Xochicalco had important trading and cultural relations with the Zapotec world, which is why some clay braziers have been discovered in excavations with representations of bats, so common among the Zapotecs.

Left. One of the treasures of the Toltec Room is the head of a bearded warrior with his coyote disguise. The most striking feature of the work is that it was made of plumbate pottery and covered with tiny pieces of mother-of-pearl.

Some stone slabs measuring time have been discovered at Xochicalco. This one, known as the stone of the four glyphs, shows the bar and dot numbering system which was vigesimal. One of the glyphs on the upper part signifies the date Four Rabbit.

Small telamons are statues typical of the Toltec world with arms raised in the attitude of holding something up since they were probably the supports of thrones or table-altars. The piece still has the rich colors that decorated the clothes of this mythical warrior.

Three monuments of carved stone with many glyphs and symbolical elements were discovered in the building of the stelae at Xochicalco. Here, the face of the god Quetzalcóatl can be seen emerging from the jaws of a serpent.

For the cult of the god Tláloc the Toltecs, like many other Mesoamerican peoples, made ritual clay vessels in the shape of jugs bearing the stylized face of the god of Rain.

Xochicalco is a city in the hot region of the state of Morelos and its name means "the place of flowers." This is why the inhabitants worshiped the god of Rain, who appears on this carved stone stelae wearing a fantastic mask over his face with a flower on his tongue.

MEXICA

At the rear of the Museum's central patio is the Mexica (Aztec) Room, the symbolical heart of the building and the culmination of a tour of the rooms dedicated to the Central Plateau that precede it. The entrance is raised, consisting of a large marble platform which connects the room with the pool and the bronze conch shell. A visit begins with the monumental sculpture of a jaguar, which was also a receptacle for the food of the gods, immediately identifying it as belonging to a stage when the gods of war dominated.

This Room is the largest and highest in the entire Museum and visitors can choose to make a tour by following the different sections or go directly to the central nave. This, like a large religious precinct, is almost a temple, with the Sun Stone or Aztec Calendar at the far end set on a dazzling altar covered with hammered copper and marble. This archaeological piece symboloizes the indigenous soul of the Mexican nation, and as it is surrounded by the other monuments it can be appreciated that this section refers to the confrontation between night and day, sun and earth, life and death. Thus, in a line beginning behind the great jaguar, there are sculptures associated with the sun and at the sides, objects to do with the earth or death.

A complete tour begins on the right side of the Room, first with descriptions of the geographical environment of the Central Plateau, the physical characteristics of the Mexicas — illustrated by sculptures of men and women — then myths and the historical evolution of the Indian nation. An outstanding exhibit is an exceptionally fine copy of the Boturini Codex or Tira de la Peregrinación which tells the story of Mexica wanderings while illustrations and famous sculptures — the Tizoc Stone for example — show the sequence of the eleven governors or *tlatoani* of México-Tenochtitlán and their exploits.

Another striking item because of its color and majesty is a replica of Moctexuma's feather headdress, which is displayed at the beginning of the next section. Here, the great model of the sacred precinct and the mural by Luis Covarrubias, with a view of the two island cities of México-Tenochtitlán and Tlatelolco set in the lake basin, evoke the grandeur of those native capitals that were conquered by the Spaniards with blood and fire in the early 16th century. This is why we only have left fragments of buildings and sculptures, silent witnesses to the way of life.

Behind the Sun Stone is the attractive model of the Market of Tlatelolco, an interpretation derived from the careful reading of Spanish chroniclers. In it we can appreciate the details of daily life: the clothing of men and women, their jewelry and ornaments, the typical pottery, the animals that served them as food and the image of the young Tezcatlipoca, who personified the god.

The following sections deal with Mexica religion, with representations of their major gods, including particularly Tláloc, god of Rain; Chicomecóatl, the goddess of Food, and Ehécatl, the lord of Wind. There are also ceremonial receptacles which were used to hold the products of human sacrifice, and the monumental figure of Coatlicue, mother of the sun.

Next is the section of minor arts, with the best examples of pottery, wooden articles and carvings in semi-precious stones. This is where visitors can see the most valuable object in the Museum's collections: an extremely fine and supremely beautiful obsidian vessel in the shape of a monkey.

The Room ends with the section on music and dance, dominated by the extraordinary statue of Xochipilli, the god of song and flowers. On display there are original wooden instrument, such as drums and xylophones. At the end there is an account of the Conquest and the destruction of a brilliant civilization that reduced the great capital, particularly its monuments and sculptures, to rubble.

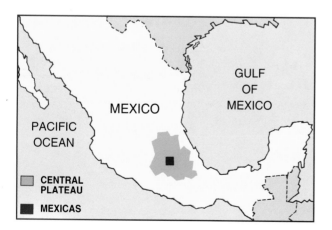

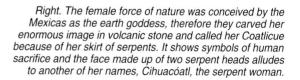

Right. The female force of nature was conceived by the Mexicas as the earth goddess, therefore they carved her enormous image in volcanic stone and called her Coatlicue because of her skirt of serpents. It shows symbols of human sacrifice and the face made up of two serpent heads alludes to another of her names, Cihuacóatl, the serpent woman.

One section of the Mexica Room is devoted to México-Tenochtitlán and its twin, Tlatelolco, which were island cities in the middle of the lake of Texcoco. The model reproduces the Ceremonial Center where the main sacred buildings of the Mexicas stood.

Xiuhtecuhtli was the god of Fire and Daylight among the Mexicas. This magnificent stone sculpture, which preserves the shell and obsidian eyes shows the god in his typical clothing.

The model of Tlatelolco market in the Mexica Room illustrates the bustling activity of the locality. Thanks to descriptions given by the Spanish conquerors we know that up to 30,000 people gathered there to exchange various goods.

The peoples of ancient Mexico venerated rattlesnakes highly. The Mexicas carved them in volcanic stone which could be highly polished.

The central section of the Room welcomes visitors with some of the finest sculptures in the Museum. In the foreground is the particularly striking sacred receptacle called Cuauhxicalli in the shape of a jaguar.

The symbol of Chapultepec park where the National Museum of Anthropology is located is a grasshopper, which the Mexicas called chapulín. The image is carved on red rock called carneolite.

The most solemn and well-made figure of the god Xochipilli comes from Tlalmanalco. It shows the god sitting cross-legged on a throne composed of flowers and butterflies sipping nectar, alluding to the patronage this deity had during the flowering of nature.

The sister of the sun, the moon, for the Mexicas was called Coyolxauhqui, a name meaning "she who decorates her face with bells." This magnificent stone sculpture, discovered near the Great Temple, refers to the fate of the goddess, who was beheaded by her brother Huitzilopochtli.

Few sculptures of the Mexica world preserve their polychrome decoration. This one combining the symbols for fire and water has the form of the god Xiuhtecuhtli, who alludes to heat, and is wearing the colors of Tláloc, god of Rain.

The Mexicas represented the universe lit by the sun's rays, and the conquests they carried out under the sun's auspices were shown on cylindrical monuments. Cuauhxicalli carved during the reign of the first Moctezuma relating the victories of his people.

Right. The most valuable treasure in the National Museum of Anthropology is the vessel of a pregnant monkey exquisitely worked in black obsidian which is an extremely fragile material. It symbolizes the action of the god of Wind who attracts clouds heavy with rain.

The Tizoc Stone is another monolith similar to the Cuauhxicalli of Moctezuma. A detail of the relief extols the triumph of a Mexica god as a Toltec warrior with the attributes of Xiuhtecuhtli and Tezcatlipoca takes the god of the enemy people by the hair and captures him.

The skill of the sculptors of the Mexica period can be appreciated in their pieces worked in very hard stone such as diorite. They took advantage of its green color to carve this naturalistic squash.

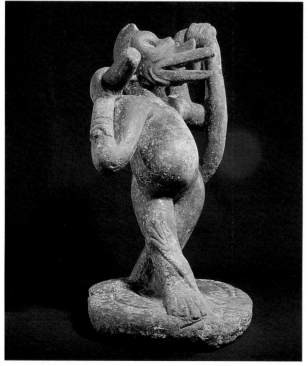

On many Mesoamerican sites there were temples dedicated to Ehécatl-Quetzalcóatl the god of Wind. This interesting sculpture of a dancing monkey which symbolically imitates the movement of the wind was discovered in Pino Suárez station of the Mexico City subway.

The temples of México-Tenochtitlán sometimes had sacred images made of clay like this life-sized portrayal of a priest of the god of Death with the ornaments and insignia of Mictlantecuhtli.

Tlapanhuéhuetl *are the vertical drums of the Indian world which were made from hollowed lengths of tree trunks. This one from Tenango del Valle is one of the finest to be preserved and is decorated with a vulture and an eagle, the symbols of war.*

Right. Above. Mexico's best known archaeological piece is the Sun Stone which was discovered in the Main Square of Mexico City in 1790. It is also called the Aztec Calendar because it tells the story of the cosmic suns and bears numerous calendar signs.

Right. Below. A Teponaxtle *is a percussion instrument with two tongues which produces resonant sounds when struck with rubber tipped drumsticks. This horizontal drum from Tlaxcala is shaped like a reclining warrior adorned with his typical ornaments and insignia.*

The calendar name of the god Xochipilli is Macuilxóchitl, "five flower" and his image decorates a stone teponaxtle. *He is shown in a stylized way as a mask made up of hands, flowers and butterflies since he is the god of Music.*

Young Mexica men prepared themselves to shine in military exploits. Stone sculpture is of the head of an eagle knight showing the man's fearless face covered by the bird helmet.

Right. Above right. The Mexicas created a ceremonial tomb, like a mausoleum, to bury the ritual sculptures that symbolized the cycles of 52 years, equivalent to our centuries. The outer facing of these mausoleums has funerary elements such as crossed bones and human skulls in profile.

Right. Above left. Priests of the Ehécatl-Quetzalcóatl cult were characterized by a half mask with a bird's beak, which they supposed the god used to produce wind.

Below right. In Tlatelolco it was the custom to smoke wild tobacco, for which elegant clay pipes were used. This is one of the most interesting as it is in the shape of a macaw, a bird connected with the sun.

60

Some clay braziers from Tlatelolco where aromatic substances were burned are decorated with the stylized image of the god of Heat and Fire, with a gold pectoral, necklaces of flowers and ears of corn.

Left. Above left. Women who died giving birth were considered divine and were called Chihuateteo. They were imagined as ghostly beings with claws poised ready to attack.

Left. Above right. The double pyramid dedicated to Huitzilopochtli and Tláloc in the Great Temple was rebuilt many times by different Mexica governors. This stone commemorates the work begun by Lord Tizoc and finished by Ahuizotl in the year "8 Reed."

Wood must have been the favorite material of Mexica sculptors. Unfortunately, because of its perishable nature very few examples survive today. One is this charming figure of the goddess of Fertility which still has its eyes and teeth of shell.

For indigenous artists, the sculptures they carved in stone had to come as near to reality as possible, therefore they incrusted pieces of shell and obsidian in their eyes and mouth, which give figures great vitality.

Left. The coyote was considered as one of the animals associated with the god Tezcatlipoca, not only because of its ferocity but also its reputed sexual prowess. The Mexicas reproduced it in their sculptures, giving it a sacred character, which is why they covered the body with hair and feathers.

CULTURES OF OAXACA

Several indigenous cultures flourished in the ancient region of Oaxaca, of which the Zapotecs and Mixtecs were the most important. A visit to this Room begins with an elegant composition of an urn of the goddess 13 Serpent and the replica of a wall with stepped fret mosaic. These synthesize the ancient art of Oaxaca.

A large map shows the location of the main archaeological sites in the region, of which Monte Albán and Mitla are the most attractive because of their magnificent state of preservation. The Room is divided into two sections, the first dedicated to archaeological finds that illustrate the evolution of the Zapotec people, and the second to the splendor of the Mixed world.

The tour continues with the oldest phases excavated in the Central Valleys of Oaxaca, with dates going back to 2000 B.C., describing a way of village life called the pre-Classic. This was the time of agricultural societies and the appearance of the first ceremonial centers. The vessels and figurines come from such localities as San José Mogote and Guadalupe, and the large showcases hold evidence of the emergence of Monte Albán I, which occurred in 600 B.C. There are elegant urns with human faces and the vessels of grey pottery that identify the art of Oaxaca.

One wall with reproductions of the "dancers" bas-reliefs reminds us of the dominance that this Indian capital in the Central Valleys exercised ever since its beginning, brutally sacrificing opponents. Some of these original stone tablets are nearby and connect the visit to the section on Monte Albán II (200 B.C. to 200 A.D.). It was during this period that the astronomical observatory was built and exquisite items were produced: the temple with the macaw, the large urns with human faces and the splendid mask of the Bat God made of jade mosaic.

The greatest era of Monte Albán and the Zapotec culture was during the Classic (200-900 A.D.) and a large painting shows the city at this time with its main plaza surrounded by platforms and buildings whose characteristic architectural feature is the vertical wall with double scapular slabs. The showcases illustrate the quality achieved by artisans in clay, of which the large polychrome urn is the best example. The most complete tombs, decorated with murals, belong to this period. The most attractive feature of the Room is a reconstruction of Tomb 104 with its original funerary offerings located on an underground level.

The final section, devoted to the Zapotecs, holds extraordinary examples of carved stone stele which commemorate conquests made by Monte Albán, and in the garden there is a reproduction of Tomb 7 where the Mixtec treasure of jewelry in gold, silver, pearls, turquoise, etc. was discovered.

The following section of the tour shows the typical characteristics of this culture, which flourished during the post-Classic (900-1524 A.D.). It was distinguished by its native books or codices on strips of deerskin, its polychrome pottery with refined decoration such as the tripod vessel of Quetzalcóatl, and in particular by the work of its gold and silversmiths who created magnificent ornaments of these precious metals. One showcase holding these Museum treasures is devoted to these artists.

The Mixtecs also worked in obsidian, turquoise mosaic, jade, rock crystal and other valuable materials, which is why the last showcases in the Room contain examples of this fine work by native craftsmen in the form of necklaces, masks, curious spatulas and stylized animal figures. The visit ends with the story of the Conquest of Oaxaca and the subjection of its peoples to the Spaniards. A notable feature here is a reproduction of the Cuilapan Slab which shows the strange way the two cultures intermingled.

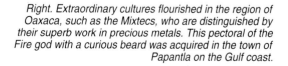

Right. Extraordinary cultures flourished in the region of Oaxaca, such as the Mixtecs, who are distinguished by their superb work in precious metals. This pectoral of the Fire god with a curious beard was acquired in the town of Papantla on the Gulf coast.

On entering the Oaxaca Room we meet the world of the Mixtecs and Zapotecs who created beautiful ritual and funerary objects, on display throughout the exhibition.

Lip plugs were ornaments worn exclusively by the warriors of Mexico. A circular cut was made below the lips for them to be inserted. This gold piece ends in the head of the god Ehécatl-Quetzalcóatl.

68

Pectoral combining the work of Mixtec goldsmiths with small turquoise mosaic. It represents a chimalli *or war shield which has a stepped fret design in the center, four aligned arrows and several bells hanging from it. From Yanhuitlán, state of Oaxaca.*

Left. Above left. Model of a temple at Monte Albán, composed of an original building with cylindrical columns and a sloping roof. In its inner patio there is a macaw.

Left. Above right. The Zapotecs of Monte Albán erected stone stelae where they carved pictures of their victories over other peoples and also the sacrifice of captured warriors. This stele comes from Building "E."

Left. Below left. The most complete and perfect polychrome vessel from the Mixtec world is this tripod pot from Nochixtlán, Oaxaca. Scenes of Quetzalcóatl worship are shown on it in the style of a codex.

Left. Below right. The Mixtecs produced jugs of various designs, and this is one of the most important because in the mouth of the vessel there is a deer's head with a tubular spout. Like in native books, ceramic painters used nay colors.

In a funerary offering at Monte Albán archaeologists discovered a support or pedestal modeled in clay which represents a section of the human skeleton, including the hip and part of the spinal column.

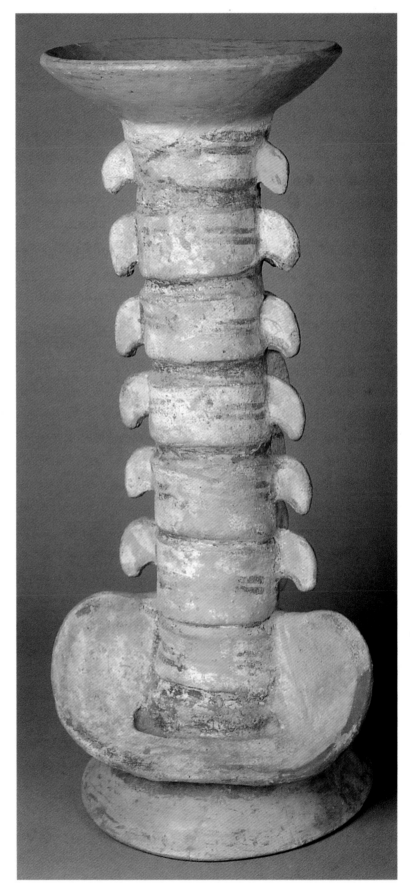

Alfonso Caso spent many seasons exploring Monte Albán, discovering more than one hundred tombs. A full-sized reproduction of Tomb 104, with copies of its mural paintings stands in the Museum. Inside is the original offering.

In the first stage of Monte Albán (600 B.C.) the Building of the Dancers was constructed and covered by curious stone slabs with relief carvings of captives sacrificed by the Zapotecs. The reproduction of one wall of the building is on display in the Museum.

Two tombs dedicated to governors of the locality were discovered at Zaachila, Oaxaca, some decades ago. This delicate brightly colored vessel comes from the treasures recovered. It has a small humming bird on one of its edges, symbolizing the god of the Sun drinking blood.

The Zapotecs produced effigy vessels known as urns showing their many deities. In this case it is goddess "1 F" who has the aspect of a nocturnal bird, represented by an owl.

Left. The Oaxaca region, especially the Valleys, has excellent deposits of clay which provided the skillful potters with magnificent raw material which they used to model large urns like this polychrome jaguar, symbol of the Zapotec capital.

Another ritual vessel discovered in the Zaachila tombs is this drinking vessel in the shape of a human skull with red markings on it which represent drops of blood or stylized hands.

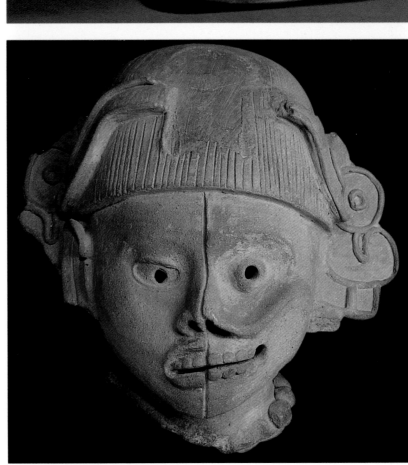

The Zapotecs too expressed the concept of duality with figures like this one from Soyaltepec, in which half of the face is fleshless, symbolizing death, while the other part is alive.

The Mixtecs were fond of the stepped fret as a decorative element, and the design is thought to represent the movement of a snake. Polychrome plate from Zaachila with stepped frets on the sides and the head of a stylized animal at the bottom.

Whistling jug. In the part that connects the vessel with the figure there is a musical instrument which emits notes with the pressure of water. A warrior with his weapons has a strange face covered in wrinkles.

One of the most striking items from Monte Albán is the mask of the Bat God composed of skillfully cut pieces of jade, brought to life with eyes and teeth of shell.

Some urns from the Early phase of Monte Albán look like fantastic masks. On this one there is the face of a deity with an enormous nose like a beak. From the Temple "7 Deer."

The Zapotecs also worshiped Xipe-Totec, the patron of metalworking to whom victims were sacrificed and then flayed. Potters modeled the deity with the face hollowed out, evoking human skin, and holding a sphere and the head of a decapitated victim.

Polychrome effigy pot showing a combination of deities where face decoration and ornaments identify Xochipilli-Macuilxochitl as patron of flowering and Xiuhtecuhtli, the warmth of the earth.

This large effigy urn was recovered from Tomb 113 at Monte Albán with the head of the Bat God with an elegant undulating neck adornment and curious eye rings like a domino mask. The large ears are integrated into the upper part of the vessel.

Left. Some of the urns that accompanied funerary offerings discovered in the tombs of Monte Albán are complex. By assembling molded sections, the potters created elaborate costumes and headdresses like this one, which reproduces the head of a jaguar.

Among the Zapotecs, the Old God also reigned over fire and heat. On this small urn, the figure is covered with clothing and wears a headdress in pastillage and incision.

The Mixtec ceremonial vessel which combine their shape with the effigy of certain gods are known as xantiles, and are one of the steps in thee-dimensional clay sculpture. This example shows the combination of the gods Xochipilli and Xiuhtecuhtli once more.

Above right. At the entrance to the Oaxaca Room stands one of the best preserved Zapotec urns. It is of the goddess "13 Serpent" with her calendar name on her garments.

A pair of figures was also found in Tomb 113 of Monte Albán which probably represent priests in a strange attitude, showing the palms of their hands to viewers.

Left. Like all Mesoamerican peoples, the Mixtecs believed that the underworld was the realm of the dead, and this god with a skeletal body reigned over it. His figure was created masterfully to decorate this funerary vessel from the tombs of Zaachila.

Some of the urns from Phase II of Monte Albán are the most naturalistic examples of Early Zapotec art to survive, and this piece is the finest. The face, believed to be the portrait of an real person, is wearing a complex zoomorphic headdress.

GULF COAST CULTURES

Three great cultures flourished in the Gulf Coast region of Mexico, in pre-hispanic times: during the pre-Classic, the Olmec (1500-600 B.C.); that of central Veracruz (600 B.C.-1300 A.D.) and the Huastec (600 B.C.- 1521 A.D.), each one with its specific section in this Room.

The Olmecs chose the jungle region crossed by great rivers in the south of Veracruz, close to Tabasco, as their home. There, in early times, they founded the most ancient ceremonial centers in Mesoamerica, of which La Venta is the best preserved today. Although their architecture was of clay, the material they used to build their pyramids, they chose hard volcanic stone such as basalt to create spectacular monuments. This was obtained in the Los Tuxtla area in Veracruz, from where it was transported with great effort on tree trunks and rafts to different sites over 60 miles away.

Using chisels and axes of diorite, a very hard stone, they carved monumental sculptures that characterize their artistic style. Examples in this Room are two colossal heads from San Lorenzo and other pieces of a symbolic or ceremonial nature, with the statue known as "the wrestler" of a man of the time symbolizing power and outstanding in its strength and perfection. Other ritual pieces from the Olmec world are displayed in cases where in addition to pottery with stylized decoration there are the chubby childlike figures of the type called "Baby Face". The Olmecs were extraordinary traders who traveled enormous distances to obtain stones of high value, especially jade, magnetite, quartz, etc. with which they carved figurines, beads for bracelets and necklaces and lovely pectorals bearing the image of supernatural beings with feline features. A special mention should be made of the ritual masks which are the purest expression of the artistic perfection attained by Olmec lapidaries.

The fragment of Stele C from Tres Zapotes, with the numbering system of bars and dots synthesizes the knowledge that this people left to the cultures that followed them.

The next section of the Room is dedicated to the peoples that lived in central Veracruz. Over the course of time these gave great continuity to the evolutionary process which links the village societies of the pre-Classic to the ceremonial centers of the Classic. Cultures such as Remojadas flourished, which produced distinctive pottery and figurines finished with patches and sections in black bitumen; or traditions such as that of the "smiling head" figurines which today are thought to illustrate rituals in which psychotropic substances were ingested.

El Tajín was the main city in the Classic period of Veracruz, and the room holds an idealized model of its principal building: the Pyramid of the Niches. In central Veracruz the cult of the ritual ballgame was practiced intensively, for which the peoples created curious sculptures known as yokes, palms and axes which are believed to celebrate the lively game with their shapes.

The Huastec culture is illustrated in the final section of the room, and the statue known as The Adolescent exemplifies the sculptural tradition of the Huastecs, in which we see men and women associated with fertility cults. This culture had a long evolution which went through all the stages of Mesoamerican development. Items dating from the pre-Classic include female figurines of a ritual nature and vessels; from the Classic and post-Classic there are magnificent anthropomorphic and zoomorphic vessels decorated in shades of red and black. A special cabinet holds the shell ornaments that were a distinguishing mark of the Huastecs, especially the magnificent pectorals that resemble the pages of codices in their detailed relief. In their final phase the Huastecs were conquered by the Mexicas, and it was then that a hybrid style of art developed in which sculptures of gods and fantastic beings were produced.

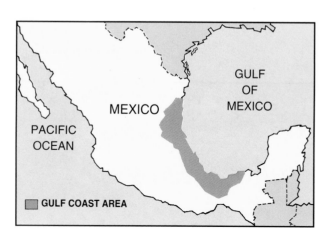

GULF COAST AREA

Right. One of the most vigorous examples of Early Gulf coast art is this Olmec sculpture of a wrestler.

The Olmec section of the Gulf Coast Room opens with a choice collection of stone sculptures made around 1000 years B.C. by the people who inhabited the low jungles of Veracruz and Tabasco.

Also from La Venta is this female figurine with traces of the cinnabar originally covering it. The most interesting feature of it is the magnetite mirror worn as a pectoral.

Colossal heads are the purest expression of Olmec stone art. The Museum has two of those found in San Lorenzo, Veracruz. This is number 4, of a governor with a helmet-like head covering.

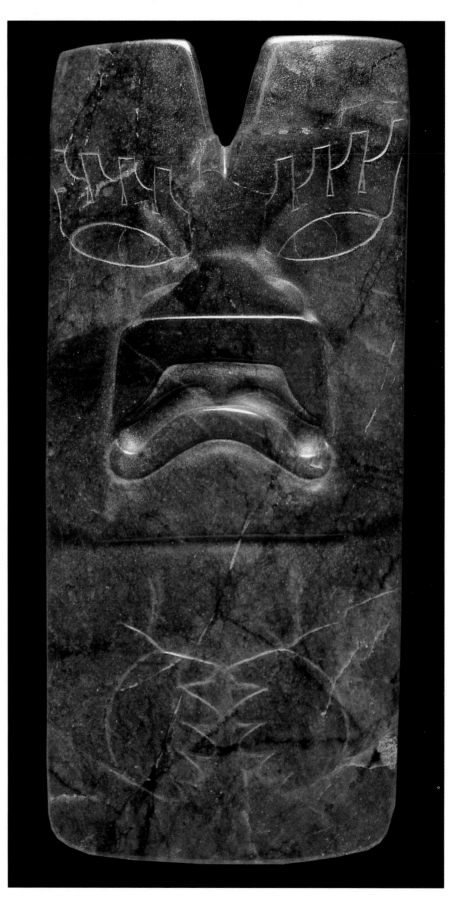

Left. One of the most sensational Olmec finds was made on the archaeological site of La Venta, Tabasco: this offering in which 16 human figurines carved of differently shaded green stone are grouped in front of six slim celts standing like stelae.

Left. Below left. The Olmecs venerated deformed persons, considering them supernatural. This is why they carved images of them in semiprecious stones such as jadeite.

Left. Below right. Olmec culture spread to various regions of Mesoamerica. Their presence in central Mexico was revealed by this remarkable head with the features and deformed skull typical of this Gulf coast people, discovered in Tenango, State of Mexico.

Outstanding among the Olmec style items are celts or plaques carved of green stone and engraved with a supernatural being that combines feline features with those of a reptile, probably a crocodile. This piece is of an extraordinary face with a double upper lip and a V shaped cut in the head.

The Olmecs venerated a thickset person with a deformed
skull as exemplified by this hollow "Baby Face" figurine.
Because of its expression and the lack of adult sexual
organs it has been interpreted as representing a man
with Down's syndrome.

Some of the most important cults in Mesoamerica emerged among the Olmecs, in particular serpent worship as shown on Stele 19 from La Venta, where the sculptor carved the sacred animal and the priest representing it in fine relief.

Some of the best examples of Olmec art have been found in the state of Guerrero such as this realistic mask which still has traces of the cinnabar used to color it.

Left. The section devoted to the Huastec culture in the Gulf Coast Room has a collection of magnificent sculptures of which the most outstanding is this adolescent.

Left. Below left. When the Mexicas conquered the Huastec region they introduced their style of sculpture. This sandstone figure of the goddess Xilonen, the patroness of corn, is one of the best examples. From Tuxpan, Veracruz.

Left. Below right. This stone, which in its time must have served as a table-altar, comes from Tepetzintla, Veracruz. It shows a god of the earth and night associated with Ehécatl-Quetzalcóatl, the Wind god. It possibly symbolizes Tlahuizcalpantecuhtli, Venus, the morning star.

One of the best examples of the clay sculpture produced by craftsmen of central Veracruz in the Classic period (300-900 A.D.) is this figure of a young man wearing a flayed human skin and mask in homage to Xipe-Totec.

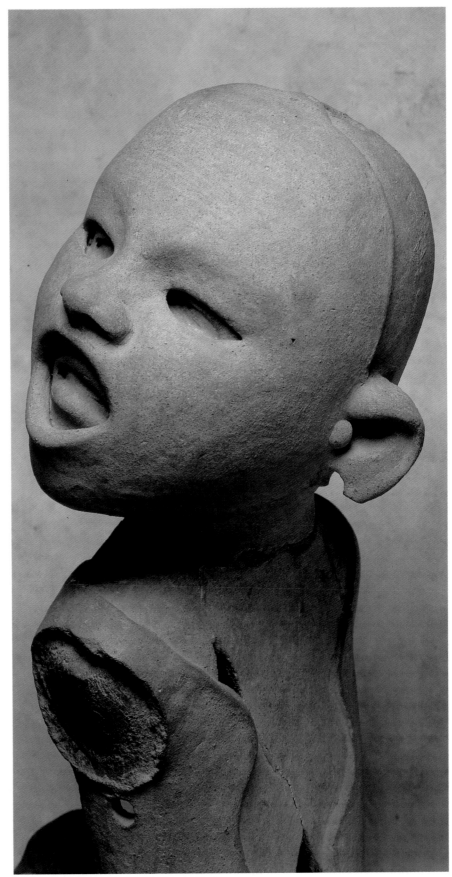

At the height of the Tajín culture in central Veracruz the cult of the ballgame grew tremendously. Extraordinary stylized human heads with ritual insignia were carved during this time such as this ceremonial axe of a man with a fish on his head.

The curved so-called yokes carved of very compact stone decorated with animals and human figures have been interpreted as stylized representations of the hip protectors worn by ballgame players.

The art of central Veracruz reached a high level of perfection in the elegant sculptures called palms. This one of two arms and joined hands emphasizes ritual mutilation.

Some of the most enigmatic sculptures from central Veracruz are known as ceremonial padlocks. They may symbolize the emblems that priests carried in their hands.

The most famous Huastec statue is this extremely stylized one of a young man. He is naked, with complicated designs on certain parts of his body relating to corn.

The Huastec adolescent carries a small human figure on his back, probably a child, which has led researchers to believe that the statue may represent Quetzalcóatl.

Right. The inhabitants of central Veracruz had very good clay available, which they used to create high quality statues. This modeled female figure, one of the best examples, is of a young woman with a naked torso.

The smiling figurines are typical of Gulf coast art toward the end of the Classic period (500-900 A.D.). Their happy expressions may be related to rituals in which psychotropic substances were consumed.

Below left. Alabaster is a stone resembling marble that was in great demand among the peoples of the Gulf coast. Vessels carved of this have been discovered in ceremonial burials on the Isla de Sacrificios, Veracruz, which show such animals as monkeys.

The Museum has the best example of polychrome ceramic dating from the Late Gulf coast era: this pot found at Los Otates, Veracruz decorated with two undulating centipedes.

In Castillo de Teayo near Tuxpan, Veracruz, there was a
Mexica colony which controlled this part of the Gulf coast.
From here is the Quetzalcóatl Stele on which the image
of the god seem to be blowing in the wind.

Stone slabs were carved with beautiful reliefs describing ritual
self-mutilation. This one from Huilozintla shows a priest of
Quetzalcóatl piercing his tongue with a rod.

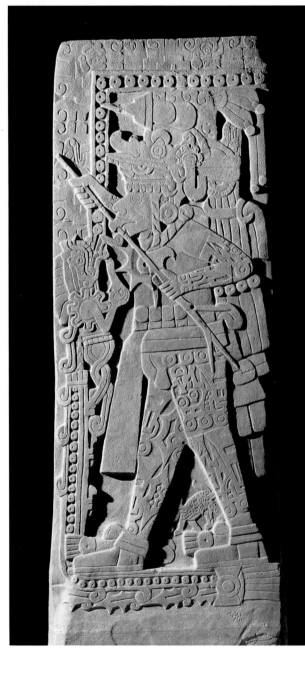

101

In the last days of the ancient Indian world many groups shared beliefs and created similar figures of gods. Such is the case of this large brazier from southern Veracruz with the head of Tláloc repeating the ceremonial mask, adornments and headgear typical of central Mexico.

Above left. The figures of Huehuetéotl, the old god of fire, take on the personality of the different groups that worshiped him. This one from Cerro de las Mesas, Veracruz is of a bent old man with a pointed beard supporting a brazier on his head.

Some of the "smiling face" figurines from the Gulf coast have jointed arms. This may mean that at one time they were clothed and flexible limbs were necessary in order to dress them.

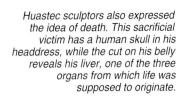
Huastec sculptors also expressed the idea of death. This sacrificial victim has a human skull in his headdress, while the cut on his belly reveals his liver, one of the three organs from which life was supposed to originate.

MAYAS

Maya civilization covered an extensive region in the south of Mesoamerica, as shown by the large relief map at the beginning of the room. In the mural illustrating the geographical environment the artist Luis Covarrubias accurately captures the numerous ecosystems of the region, with two major areas: on one hand the Lowlands, with lush tropical rain forests such as those of El Petén in Guatemala and Lacandon country in Mexico, and the plain of the Yucatán peninsula with its underground rivers and scarce heights. On the other hand are the Highlands, characterized by high valleys set in mountain chains surrounded by mixed forest.

Maya cultural development is divided into three great stages: the pre-Classic, from 1500 to 150 B.C., which is when the first villages arose, with an economy based on the cultivation of corn. In its Late phase, from 300 B.C. on, the full integration of the Maya civilization came about with the beginning of hieroglyphic writing and later when Izapa developed, the stele-altar complex became firmly established, and the room contains the finest examples of this from the site.

The Classic period (300-900 A.D.) marks the peak of this civilization which left very special remains on archaeological sites such as Palenque, Yaxchilán, Bonampak and others. Most of the objects exhibited in the room belong to this period, and especially noteworthy among them for their aesthetic quality are the stele from Yaxchilán and the figurines and pottery from the island of Jaina. During the Classic period a great impulse was given to the knowledge of astronomy, the development of writing and the entire range of aesthetic expressions.

The post-Classic period (900-1521 A.D.) began with a radical change in art, especially in the cities located in the north of the Yucatán peninsula, due to the presence of Toltecs from the Central Plateau. We know several historical accounts collected after the Conquest which describe constant wars between Maya states. These led to a period of cultural decline that is demonstrated by the reduction and lower quality of artistic works, contrasting with the surge of commerce in all the northern area. The site best illustrating this is Tulum in the state of Quintana Roo.

The room begins with a description of the physical characteristics of the ancient Mayas, who set themselves apart from other groups with their artificially flattened skulls, filed teeth, induced crossed-eyes and scarification.

The objects dating from the Classic period, genuine masterpieces, show the Mayas' relationship with plants, animals, with their very realistic or exquisitely stylized representations of flora and fauna. The Mayas expressed themselves in figurines, ceramic vessels, sculptures, jade and mother-of-pearl jewelry, distinguishing their art with refined techniques and elegant style that makes us recognize them as one of the peoples that made most contributions to Mesoamerican plastic art.

In the central section of the room there is a colorful mural by Rina Lazo showing the complex mythology of the Mayas and its relationship with everyday life. This creates the atmosphere for displays of temple facades, objects telling the story of ceremonial activities and trade, all leading up to the tomb from the Temple of the Inscriptions with its extraordinary treasure of jade, including the magnificent mask of Lord Pakal.

In the garden stand faithful reproductions of the painted rooms of Bonampak and the facade of the principal temple of Hochoob. Back in the room, a mural by Raúl Anguiano shows the myth of man being created from corn dough. The final section is devoted to the post-Classic period, the main attraction being the gold jewelry recovered from the Sacred Well of Chichén Itzá and select examples of art dating from the final period of ancient Maya civilization.

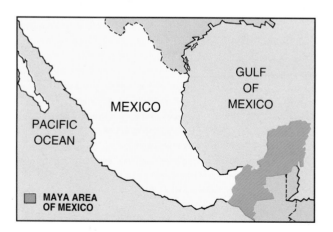

Right. The highest political rank among the Mayas was held by the Halach Uinic, *a semi-divine governor who appeared before his people wearing impressive jade ornaments, elaborate clothes and an enormous headdress as shown by this throned figurine from Jaina.*

Left. Above left. Jaina, an island off the coast of Campeche, was a ritual center where many burials dating from the Classic Maya period have been found with hundreds of realistic clay figurines such as this one.

Left. Above right. Warriors wore padded cotton armor and carried shields, as shown by this figurine with a deformed skull and an enormous pectoral of split conch shell.

Left. Below left. Some of the Jaina figurines are full of movement. Although this one is commonly known as "the orator" some experts think it could also be a dancer.

Left. Below right. Many details of everyday life are shown in Jaina figurines. This one is of an elegantly dressed woman holding a skein of yarn and a spindle.

Ever since it was discovered this figure has popularly been called "the cowboy" because of its large hat. Its attraction is the famous Maya blue of its long shirt.

Above left. The middle section of the Maya Room contains one of the best collections of sculpture from different sites, notably the stelae and lintels from Yaxchilán.

Lintel 53 from Yaxchilán shows ritual scenes involving one of the last governors of this city, "Jaguar Shield," wearing an elaborate costume and adornments of quetzal feathers. Opposite him is his wife "Wind Skull."

Left. Below left. Some figurines from Jaina show items of female clothing such as the quechquémitl which is still worn today. In addition, this piece shows the practice of scarification — designs on the face in deep scars for purposes of beauty.

Left. Below right. Maya weavers used backstrap looms to produce beautiful garments of cotton and other vegetable fibers as shown by this clay figurine which has also been interpreted as representing the goddess Ix Chel.

109

The tablet from the Temple of the Cross in Palenque is composed of three large limestone slabs showing ceremonial acts of the reign of Pakal and his descendent Cham Balum. The balance between the human figure and the cartouches of glyphs can be appreciated on this segment, which is the left-hand part.

Above. In the garden outside the Maya Room is the full-sized reproduction of the temple of Hochoob with the architectural decoration typical of the Chenes style. The ornamentation completely covers the facade of the building and the entrance imitates the jaws of a gigantic reptile.

One of the major attractions of the architectural section of the Maya Room is a large stucco facade. On the middle section is the image of the Sun god flanked by two old deities who hold calendar symbols in their hands.

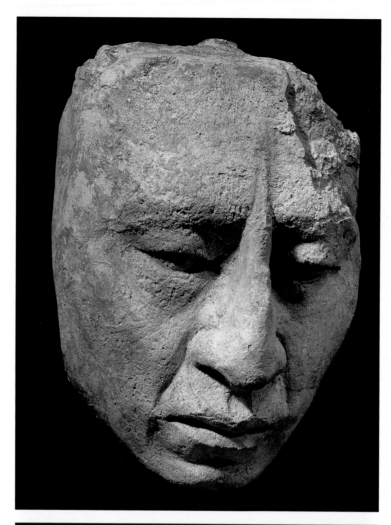

This tiny sculpture was carved from an animal bone and was the head of the scepter of a Halach Uinic. It shows one of the governors of the Maya world wearing a large headdress of quetzal plumes and a jaguar pelt indicating his royal rank.

Above left. Some of the stucco sculptures from Palenque, Chiapas illustrate the quality of workmanship achieved by the artists of the Classic Maya world who captured the facial features of local governors most realistically.

The coast of Quintana Roo is where the finest examples of the descending god associated with corn worship are found. This ceremonial vessel of polychrome stucco from Dzibanché shows the god holding flowers.

Lintel 26 from Yaxchilán, on which governor "Jaguar Shield" is receiving the head of a feline as a symbol of power and rank from his wife "Fish Fist." Both have the typical deformed skulls of Maya nobles.

This clay vessel in the shape of a jaguar head comes from the state of Tabasco. Like other Mesoamerican peoples, the Mayas regarded this animal as a symbol of war and the power of governors.

Late post-Classic (1300-1521) pottery from Mayapán and other Maya cities is distinguished by magnificent modeling and painting. This is Chac, the Wind god, holding ritual spheres.

Right. One of the sculptures most representative of the late Classic period on the Yucatán peninsula is this one known as "the Queen of Uxmal." A human face emerges from the gaping jaws of a stylized serpent.

The Museum has a collection of stucco glyphs from the Forgotten Temple at Palenque known as "head variants." The head of an old man has the numeral five on the left and on the right a huinal or period of 20 years symbolized by a frog's head.

Below right. Characteristic features of the Mexica-Maya style of the Early post-Classic period on the Yucatán peninsula are telamons which supported platforms or altars. This one from the Temple of the Tigers at Chichén Itzá is wearing a jaguar pectoral.

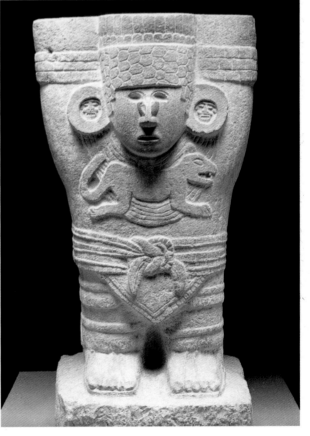

The pyramid known as *The Castle* at Chichén Itzá is aligned to mark the passage of the sun at the equinoxes. This disk covered in turquoise mosaic, with four feathered serpents, must have been part of the sacred symbolism between the supreme god Kukulkán and the sun.

Below left. Some of the platforms at Chichén Itzá show animals associated with war and human sacrifice. On this stone, a jaguar is about to devour a heart.

The oldest Maya item, acquired by the Museum in the 19th century, is the Chac-Mool from inside the Venus Platform at Chichén Itzá which was given this name by the French explorer Le Plongeon.

Several cylinders with braziers on top were discovered during explorations of the Temple of the Cross and the Temple of the Leafy Cross at Palenque. Some of them, like this one, show the Sun god of the Mayas.

This tiny jade figurine of the Mayan Sun god was found along with other ritual items in the sarcophagus of Lord Pakal at Palenque.

The National Museum of Anthropology has a magnificent replica of Pakal's tomb at Palenque. Here, visitors can appreciate the inside of the burial chamber and the reliefs on the stone slab covering the sarcophagus.

Right. This impressive funerary mask covered with jade mosaic was included in the rich offerings Lord Pakal was buried with in the Temple of the Inscriptions of Palenque. It represents the face of the governor, with his deformed skull, lined forehead and filed teeth.

Below left. Some Maya pieces indicate phallus worship. Perhaps the best example is this figure of a young man from Cumpich, Yucatán.

The imagination of Maya potters led them to use various forms and techniques. Here, a highly polished vessel in the shape of a snail is combined with the hand-modeled figure of an old man emerging from inside who possibly represents a dwarf or spirit.

Another building reproduced in the garden outside the Maya Room is the Temple of the Frescoes of Bonampak whose murals were copied by the artist Rina Lazo. This detail from room two shows prisoners of war being punished.

Jade, a material highly appreciated by the Mayas and other Mesoamerican peoples symbolized the most precious that existed in nature, therefore it was the exclusive property of the ruling class. This pectoral shows a Halach Uinic in profile holding a ceremonial rod in both arms.

Before the powerful cities of the Classic period arose there were some communities in Chiapas such as Chiapa de Corzo where strikingly original pottery vessels have been found which are believed to be associated with the worship of the Wind god.

The Chinkultik disk is a ballcourt marker carved with a player wearing a waist protector and elaborate feather headdress. The dynamic figure is shooting the ball with his hip and is surrounded by a circle of hieroglyphs which include the date 591 A.D.

The Codz Pop of Kabah is one of the most striking examples of Maya architecture, with its facade covered in masks of Chac, the god of Rain. This sample illustrates the technique of joining together sections of carved stone mosaic fashion.

When Alberto Ruz discovered the burial chamber of Pakal in the Temple of the Inscriptions there was this stucco head of a young Maya noble with a deformed skull and elongated profile which is accentuated by the elaborate hairstyle.

To hunt successfully, the Mayas disguised themselves as the animals they went after. This is the central motif of the polychrome plate showing a group of hunters using blowpipes to bring down deer.

The Maya pottery most appreciated for its high quality is the polychrome ware on which artists painted members of the elite, identified by their elaborate clothing and feather adornments.

Right. On this limestone slab from Jonuta, Tabasco, Maya artists carved a priest performing a ritual. He has a thin beard and wears a phallic symbol on his chest while on his back is the realistic image of a macaw.

Maya ceramic traditions of the Classic era are exemplified by the tripod vessels with mammiform supports and the outer edge decorated with polychrome designs.

Among the most remarkable techniques used by Maya potters to decorate ceramic ware was engraving the clay before firing, which enabled them to create scenes as if in relief of high-ranking persons and hieroglyphs.

Polychrome bowl decorated with a curious scene: a naked man is inserting a cannula into his rectum perhaps for medical purposes.

In the transitional period between the Classic and post-Classic periods pizarra pottery became popular on the Yucatán peninsula. Light yellowish in color, it was finely incised with geometric motifs resembling the facades of buildings.

There were basically three deeply contrasting cultures in the enormous reaches of northern Mexico. Arid America, characterized by the absolute dependence on hunting and gathering of the groups which lived there; Marginal Mesoamerica, which shared features with the great civilizing area that was its neighbor, with its mixed economy in which agriculture played a significant role, and Oasis America, actually a southern extension of the cultures of the southwest United States, whose artistic expressions are very different from those of Mesoamerica.

The sections of the room devoted to the Northern Cultures illustrate these different developments, and the modern items are recreations of murals by the Kivas of Kuaua, New Mexico, U.S.A.

The first section, Arid America, displays the cultural tradition of the desert, going back to about 8000 B.C. Here we can see the basic pattern of economy based on hunting and gathering which lasted into historical times to be described meticulously by the conquering Spanish and even 19th-century travelers. The items exhibited come mainly from La Candelaria cave in the state of Coahuila, and even though they were for funerary purposes, we can surmise that they were also used in daily life. Human remains, some mummified, still have ornaments they used to weave into their hair and many items of clothing, especially sashes and cloaks with interesting geometric decoration. There are weapons whose blades of chipped stone still have their wooden hafts, ornaments and jewelry with snake vertebrae or shell beads, basketwork and hunting weapons.

The following section illustrates the agricultural tradition which was carried on with great difficulty in the north of Mexico. Specialists call it Marginal Mesoamerica, and it covered an extensive region from the Bajío to the mountains of Querétaro, San Luis Potosí, Zacatecas, Durango and the mountains of Tamaulipas. In these lands, where environmental conditions permitted the development of agriculture or other productive activity such as mining, communities arose that shared many elements with Mesoamerica.

There are also interesting examples of traditional pottery which exemplify the styles of Guanajuato and San Luis Potosí, where there was a close relationship with the Toltec world: sites such as Toluquilla and Ranas the mountains of Querétaro, provide rich information about the ballgame cult, and not only courts have been discovered but also sculptures of yokes, which are evidence of contact with the Gulf Coast and the city of Teotihuacán which needed the valuable cinnabar from its mines.

Paquimé in Chihuahua, better known as Casas Grandes, is the most important site of Oasis America. At the beginning it had influences from the Mogollon Indians, a people living in the southwestern United States, and later from the Anasazi. The site is characterized by its enormous dwelling complexes built of adobe, and the inhabitants practiced agriculture using irrigation channels. Casas Grandes was at its height between 1100 and 1300 A.D., when pyramidal bases were also built and there were courts for the ballgame. This culture is distinguished by its elegant pottery decorated with geometric disks in which shades of red and black contrast with the cream-colored ground. The finest examples are displayed in the room, together with copper ornaments and pendants of turquoise mosaic, all of them discovered in archaeological excavations carried out in the locality.

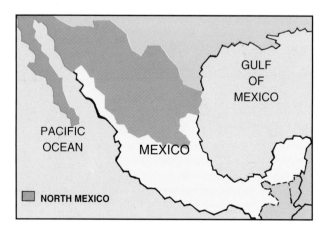

Right. The inhabitants of Paquimé, the adobe city in the north of Chihuahua also known as Casas Grandes, produced these anthropomorphic vessels combining human forms with the geometric designs they covered their faces and bodies with.

Above left. Desert vegetation characterized by thorny xerophytes formed the environment where groups of hunters and collectors developed who deposited their dead in La Candelaria cave, Coahuila.

Archaeological studies carried out at Paquimé have shown that the inhabitants of this city had bird farms which were very important in the development of the Casas Grandes culture. Pictures of them decorated elegant clay vessels.

Left. Below left. This vessel is erotic in nature, representing sexual union between a man and a woman. A notable feature is the large size of the female figure, whose body is decorated with geometric designs.

Left. Below right. Anthropomorphic vessels in the style of Casas Grandes include items that show expressions of great surprise.

In pre-Hispanic times, the archaeological site of San Miguel de Allende lay in the area known as Marginal Mesoamerica. From here come these three stylized figures known as "lids" showing persons wearing large curved headdresses.

Left. Curious vessel in the Casas Grandes style of a person with a hand over his mouth in a strange gesture. The designs on his body, which symbolize the relationship of man with sacred animals are striking.

This whistling vessel from El Cóporo, Guanajuato, has a finely modeled figure at its end and a whistle inside that produces melodious sounds when water is poured in.

WEST

The culture area which covers Mexico's Pacific coast is commonly known as The West. The Room devoted to this exhibits objects from the present-day states of Guerrero, Michoacán, Guanajuato, Jalisco, Colima, Nayarit and Sinaloa. A visit begins with the mural by Luis Covarrubias which shows the extensive geographical region and explains its major ecological zones: the Coast, the Sierra Madre Occidental and the wide mesetas of the Central Plateau with their lake basins.

In this complex area, archaeologists have been able to determine cultural expressions which developed over three Mesoamerican evolutionary phases (pre-Classic, Classic and post-Classic) and which can be found in some form or another in various modern states.

One of the earliest types of pottery in Mesoamerica developed on the coast of Guerrero and during the pre-Classic, the San Jerónimo culture, with its peculiar long-headed figurines characterize village cultures. Also from this period is the Capacha culture of Colima, dating back to 1450 B.C. In the Room this can be identified by the curious vessels known as gourds (bules) with multiple globular bodies which are very similar to objects from South America, probably indicating contacts between the two regions. In Guerrero there is evidence of the Olmec culture, both in the rock paintings of Oxtotitlán and on the monumental site of Teopantecuantitlán.

Without any doubt, the best known pre-Classic culture of Western Mexico is that of Chupícuaro in Guanajuato which covered a wide area of the Bajío region. This, like other contemporary Mesoamerican sites, was a village complex where the most distinctive features are burials accompanied by offerings that include typical pottery with geometric decorations.

In the central part of the room is the rich cultural complex of the Tiro Tombs which come from these funerary deposits located in a wide region of Western Mexico. Thanks to excavations we have information about the custom of burying the dead with a collection of pottery vessels and clay figures with which this people showed their daily and ritual activities. In the many showcases there are figures of animals which illustrate the particular Mesoamerican fauna, including macaws, ducks and particularly the native dogs called *xoloitzcuintlis* which were hairless and were fattened for food. The highly stylized anthropomorphic figures show us individuals in various attitudes, with the clothing and jewelry that identified them.

The third section of the room begins with the Mezcala culture, which flourished in Guerrero, and is distinguished by small carvings in gray stone. This was used for funeral masks, models of temples and images of supernatural animals. It ends with the Purépecha (Tarascan) culture which basically spread over Michoacán. Its period of greatest flourishing was the Late pre-Classic (1300-1521 A.D.) at the same time as the Mexicas.

The Purépechas belonged to a complex state known as the Tarascan empire which was extremely warlike. Its head of government was Caltzontzin, and the capital Tzintzuntzan, where the ritual buildings called *yácatas* still stand, which are reproduced in a model.

The showcases hold the pottery characteristic of this people, and in particular an extensive collection of weapons, tools and jewelry made of copper, bronze, gold and silver which show that the Tarascans were great metalworkers. Their particular style of carving stone is characterized by geometric forms in the figures of animals and humans, thus we have a throne in the shape of a coyote. However, the most important piece in this room is the Chac-Mool from Iguatzio, a refined expression of this people's sculpture.

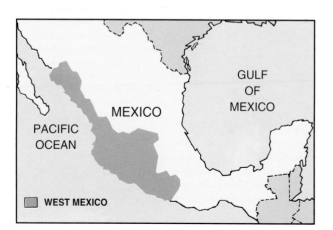

Right. Female figure, the most beautiful ceramic work from the Tiro Tombs which illustrates the harmonious concept the ancient potters of the state of Nayarit had of the human body. The naked woman wears rings of shell or metal in her ears and nose and has her hands over her abdomen, indicating that she is giving birth.

In the Tiro Tombs of Colima there are many figures of plump dogs, typically reddish in color and highly polished. This piece is particularly noteworthy because the animal is wearing a human mask, expressing the idea that man leads the souls of animals into the underworld.

The custom in West Mexico of accompanying funerary offerings deposited in the bottom of Tiro Tombs with a large number of clay sculptures or vessels enriched knowledge of everyday life. An example is this libation, in which the person is using several vessels.

Some of the vessels from Colima are of a breed of dog characteristic of ancient Mexico called xoloitzcuintli *which when adult was slim and adopted this special pose when lying down.*

Although there are no very important ruins showing the ancient architecture of the Teuchitlán tradition, the clay models from the shaft tombs of Nayarit, illustrate daily life in the region very realistically as well as the buildings that were typically of wood, rods, mud and straw.

Some female figures in the Nayarit style are known as "Chinese women" because of their small elongated eyes as can be seen from this vessel showing a naked young woman with an expression of surprise.

Right. During the Late pre-Classic (600 B.C. to 100 B.C.) the Chupícuaro culture developed in the state of Guanajuato. This is characterized by female figurines with enigmatic faces and enormous slanting eyes like coffee beans.

140

The clay animals from the state of Colima include a macaw which is a vessel with a spout in the tail. This type of pottery is distinguished by its color and high polish.

Left. This sculpture of a man from West Mexico was one of the first pieces to arrive at the Museum. The modeling is very vigorous, and the figure represents a warrior with his armor and helmet woven of vegetable fibers who is brandishing a war club in both hands.

Numerous human figures have been recovered from Tiro Tombs in the Colima region. An outstanding example is this one with the head on one hand and knee, giving the whole figure an elegant fluidity.

Left. The painter Diego Rivera and other collectors of his time were very fond of the figures from Tiro Tombs, particularly those of men wearing headdresses with several points, which they nicknamed "clowns."

Figure of a man probably playing a musical instrument or else drinking from an original vessel, which synthesizes the Nayarit style. The potter-artist stylizes limbs by elongating them and achieves a sharp contrast between the color of the face painting and the basic shade of the clay.

The relationship of the shaft tomb culture with agriculture is illustrated magnificently by these vessels that evoke the importance of squash, and which balance its globular shape with the supports of birds with long beaks.

Left. The potter-artists of Nayarit achieved not only stylization in their creations but also a touch of social satire. This is one of the best examples: an emaciated old woman with a hare lip separating the kernels from ears of corn.

The archaeological site of Huandacareo in Michoacán has yielded valuable examples of pottery which prove the presence of decorative techniques from central Mexico and the use of stuccoed and painted designs similar to those of Teotihuacán.

During the construction of the Infiernillo dam on the Balsas river, valuable archaeological material associated with the ritual life of the inhabitants of West Mexico was recovered. This is the origin of conch shells used as musical instruments that were cut out to make them very light.

Tarascan sculptors developed a style characterized by extremely geometric lines. Such is the appearance of this coyote of a phallic nature which is related to the domain of this animal and masculinity.

Some clay vessels and figures illustrate various aspects of the daily life of the peoples of West Mexico. This one is a pot carrier.

The Tarascans introduced new shapes and styles into the pottery of West Mexico, giving their vessels globular feet. The high sheen resembles wax polishing, and some of the designs were achieved by the negative technique.

From the Classic era until the time of the Mexicas, the Mezcala style developed in the state of Guerrero. Very compact stone varying in color from light gray to dark green was used to produce highly stylized masks in particular.

Various clay figures show mythical persons such as this old hunchbacked man standing on what seems to be a two-headed fish. Therefore it has been interpreted as representing the god of Fire or of Fish.

Some clay models reproduce the architecture of their time: stairways leading up to temples whose roofs made of wood and straw were supported on walls and columns. In this example, the artist placed the sacrificial stone opposite the temple.

On the upper floor are the Rooms dedicated to the main ethnic groups of modern Mexico. Following the original concept of the Museum, a visit begins with the first Room in the north which, in the present process of museum renovation is called Indian Peoples. Here there is a summary of the characteristics that these groups have today which make up an important part of the Mexican nation. It explains the elements which distinguish them: their different languages, settlement patterns, economy and their rich cultural and spiritual material present at fiestas, costume, buildings, utensils, etc.

The part on the Huichols and Coras shows cultural evidence of these groups which live in the states of Nayarit and Jalisco. The most important features are their textiles woven on backstrap looms, in which original geometric designs are the distinctive element, as well as the colorful objects they decorate with tiny beads, something introduced after the Conquest.

Present-day Purépechas live in Michoacán like their ancestors did. They continue to exploit their lake filled land, hunting and fishing and building their typical wooden mountain cabins, called *trojes*. They are extraordinarily skilled at hammered copper work, producing elaborate masks for their dances and Christmas plays.

Scattered over an extensive region in central Mexico are the Otomi-Pame, made up of various groups, particularly the Otomis. Since immemorial times this people has had to face the harsh environment of semi-desert areas by obtaining from cactuses the fiber they use to make ropes and textiles of different types, a handicraft that distinguishes them, together with carving miniatures with mother-of-pearl incrustations.

The Sierra de Puebla is inhabited mainly by Nahuas, Totonacs, Otomis and Tepehuas. It is a rich agricultural area and today the main crops are sugarcane and coffee. These groups preserve their pre-Hispanic costume to a large extent in which the *quechquémitl* of the women is very attractive, while another of their distinctive cultural elements is the manufacture of native paper from the bark of the wild fig (*amate*) tree.

The largest concentration of indigenous communities is in the south of Mexico, and the Oaxaca Room is devoted to displays of the most noteworthy objects from the culture of the more than 16 groups that survive today, with their various languages. The Zapotecs have an important place because of their nearness to the capital, and they are very well known because of their fiesta of Guelaguetza, the costume of the Tehuanas and the black pottery of Coyotepec. In the north of Oaxaca live the Chinantecs and Mazatecs whose women wear beautiful *huipiles* (shifts) which they intersperse with brightly colored ribbons. The Mixtecs are very conservative, but the richness of their *huipiles* with geometric designs and the skillful weaving of straw hats is to be admired.

The Mayas of Mexico today are illustrated in two Rooms: those who live in the lowlands in Tabasco, Chiapas and the Yucatán peninsula. Of these, the most notable for their adaptation to the rain forest environment are the Lacandons, who wear long cotton tunics and make incense burners with the faces of gods, which they use for their ceremonies. The Yucatecan Mayas fought for many years to shake off subjection. The *huipil* is the everyday garment of women, and they still perform the ancient agricultural ceremony of Cha-Chaac to bring rain. The highland Mayas are the Tzotzils, Tzeltals and Tojolabals, who make their everyday clothes of wool to protect them against the harsh conditions of the mountainous region they inhabit. Their principal fiesta is best known as the carnival of San Juan Chamula.

The tour of the Museum's ethnography section ends with the Rooms dedicated to the peoples of the Northwest and the Nahuas. The first shows the culture of the Seris, Tarahumaras, Yaquis and the Mayos, highlighting the sharp contrast between the ways of life of the inhabitants of the Sonora coast and those who live in the rugged Chihuahua mountains. These peoples have been strongly influenced by the West, but in their dances, facial decoration and in some fine items of basketwork, they demonstrate their identity.

The Nahuas, scattered over a large area of Mexico are more fully integrated into modern life. They are characterized particularly by the continuity in using their language and their spectacular fiestas and dances, introduced after the Conquest, in which people dressed as Arab princes or Christian soldiers take part.

Right. The Lowland Maya Room shows the typical dwellings of the Yucatán peninsula with walls made of sticks and straw roofs. An explanation of the techniques preparing and utilizing henequen fiber is also given.

Old techniques of working in clay are still continued in the communities of Chililico and Huejutla, Hidalgo, where even today, cooking pots and figures are made with decoration achieved by applying corn gruel.

Mural by Antonio Estrada in the Oaxaca Room illustrating the devotions of the inhabitants of indigenous communities. They not only celebrate religious festivals with processions of their most important sacred images, but also leave offerings of tiny clay animals in their fields.

In the Cora-Huichol Room, the traditional costumes of these groups can be seen, with their splendid brightly colored embroidery, in addition to their shrines with ritual equipment.

Among the traditional dances performed by the Mixtecs is the one of the "devils." It satirizes mestizos, who are supposed to have a despotic attitude towards Nahuas.

Right. The Purépechas, also known as Tarascans, live in the lake region of Michoacán. They wear garments made of wool in which dark colors predominate.

The Feather Dance is typical of contemporary Zapotecs. A remarkable feature is the agility with which the dancers perform while wearing enormous headdresses of mirrors and ostrich feathers which have been imported into Mexico since Colonial times.

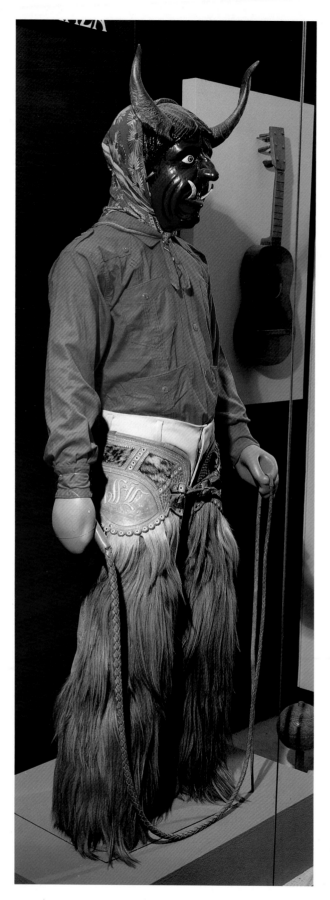

The mixing of cultures is evident in the Mexican countryside by the use of wheels and of oxen for plowing. The Zapotecs of the Central Valleys of Oaxaca commonly employ this type of cart.

The Totonacs live in central Veracruz and a neighboring area of Puebla. In their dances they wear velvet costumes with bright embroidery and wooden masks, to which they make a vow of sexual abstinence in the days prior to the dance, and headdresses that include mirrors.

The entire state of Oaxaca is an ethnographic mosaic where many linguistic groups live side by side even today: Zapotecs, Mixtecs, Chinantecs, Yalaltecs, Mixes and others. This picture shows the survival of traditional costume in some of them, especially the use of huipiles and wrap-around skirts by women.

Chinantec huipiles are composed of sections woven on back-strap looms in which geometric designs predominate. Various shades of cotton are used to make these, and brilliantly colored ribbons are applied to some sections.

The groups living in the Sierra de Puebla are Nahuas, Totonacs, Tepehuas and Otomis, who have remarkable cultural affinity due to their constant contact. However, each group preserves its own language, customs and dances.

One of the most important handicrafts among the Otomis of the Mezquital valley is weaving agave fiber. In the Room devoted to this group, the production process is explained, as well as the use of this plant as food and building material.

Traditional Mexican kitchens are based mainly on age-old ways of the pre-Hispanic world. The principal features of this Tarascan kitchen are the metates or grindstones and the adobe range with several heating holes. The comal (griddle) is placed over the largest one.

NATIONAL MUSEUM OF ANTHROPOLOGY

Project and Concept: Casa Editrice Bonechi
Publication Manager: Monica Bonechi
Cover and Graphic design: Sonia Gottardo
Layout: Alberto Douglas Scotti
Editing: Patrizia Fabbri

© Copyright by Casa Editrice Bonechi,
Via Cairoli 18b
50131 Florence, Italy

E-mail: bonechi@bonechi.it - Internet: www.bonechi.it

ISBN 88-476-0326-9

NATIONAL MUSEUM OF ANTHROPOLOGY

Project and Concept: Monclem Ediciones
Publication Manager: Concepción Cadena
Cover and Layout: Angel Escobar
Editing: Angel Escobar
Translated by David B. Castledine

© Copyright by Monclem Ediciones, S.A. de C.V.
Leibnitz 31
Col. Anzures
11590 México, D.F.-México
Tel. 55 20 81 67 - Fax 52 02 88 14

ISBN 968-6434-92 5

Printed in Italy by
Centro Stampa Editoriale Bonechi.

Distributor:
Monclem Ediciones, S.A. de C.V.
Leibnitz 31
Col. Anzures
11590 México, D.F.-México
Tel. 55 45 77 42 - 62 55 42 88
Fax 52 03 46 57

* * *

The Author
Felipe Solís, archaeologist and historian, has been curator of the Mexica collections of the National Museum of Anthropology since 1972, and in 1990 was appoined director of archaeology.
He is also a professor at the National Autonomous University, organizer of exhibitions both in Mexico and abroad and author of numerous publications about the pre-Hispanic world.

PHOTO CREDITS

Gianni Dagli Orti
4 top, 4 bottom, 7 bottom, 10, 11, 12/13 top, 13 bottom, 14, 15, 16, 17, 21, 23 top right, 24 top right, 25, 26, 29, 30 top, 31 top, 31 bottom, 32 bottom, 33 top left, 33 right, 34 top right, 34 bottom left, 35 top right, 35 bottom right, 36, 37 bottom, 39, 40 top, 41 top, 41 bottom right, 42, 43 top, 43 bottom, 44 top left, 44 top right, 45 right, 47, 48/49, 50 top, 51 top, 51 bottom, 52, 53 top, 53 bottom, 54 top, 54 bottom, 56 top, 57, 58 top, 58 bottom, 59 top, 59 bottom, 60 top, 61 top left, 61 top right, 61 bottom, 62 top left, 62 top right, 62 bottom, 63 right, 64, 65, 67, 68 top, 69, 70 top right, 72 top, 72 bottom, 73 top, 74, 75 top, 76 top, 77, 79, 80, 81, 82, 83 top left, 83 top right, 83 bottom, 84, 85, 87, 88 top, 88 bottom, 89, 90 top, 90 bottom left, 92, 93 top, 94 top, 94 bottom left, 94 bottom right, 96 top, 96 bottom, 97 right, 98 left, 98 right, 99, 100 bottom left, 100 bottom right, 101 left, 102 top left, 102 top right, 103, 105, 106 top left, 106 top right, 106 bottom right, 107, 108 top, 109, 110, 111 top, 111 bottom, 112 top left, 113 top, 114, 115 bottom right, 116 right, 116 bottom left, 116 bottom right, 117 right, 118 top, 118 bottom left, 119, 120, 121 top, 122 top, 122 bottom, 125, 126 top, 130 top, 135, 136 top, 139, 140, 141 top, 143, 146 top, 146 bottom, 148 bottom, 151, 152/153 top, 152 bottom, 154 left, 154 right, 155, 156 top, 156 bottom, 157 top, 157 bottom, 158, 159 bottom

Michel Zabé
23 top left, 23 bottom left, 24 bottom left, 30 bottom, 49 right, 55, 68 bottom, 70 bottom right, 73 bottom, 76 bottom, 95, 101 right, 108 bottom right, 115 bottom left, 117 left, 123, 129, 130 bottom left, 130 bottom right, 133 top

Agustín Estrada
34 bottom right, 50 bottom, 71, 75 bottom, 78 top, 97 left, 131, 132, 145 bottom, 148 top, 149 left

Pedro Hiriart
40 bottom left

Salvador Guillén
78 bottom

I. Groth
118 bottom right, 124 bottom, 126 bottom, 127 top, 127 bottom

Javier Hinojosa
6/7 top, 8, 9, 153 bottom, 159 top

Reyes Medina
22 top, 22 bottom, 23 bottom right, 24 top left, 27, 32 top, 34 top left, 37 top, 45 left, 56 bottom, 70 top left, 70 bottom left, 90 bottom right, 91, 93 bottom, 100 top, 102 bottom, 106 bottom left, 112 top right, 112 bottom, 113 bottom, 121 bottom, 124 top, 133 bottom, 136 bottom, 137 top, 137 bottom, 138, 147, 149 right

Archivo Hachette Latinoamérica
5 top, 108 bottom left, 115 top, 141 bottom, 142, 144, 145 top